How to Use This Book

This book is a guide to safety for international travelers; it also serves to promote the comfort and well-being of the overseas traveler. Read the table of contents first, to see what each section is about. Then refer to the appropriate section for discussion of each topic as it may apply to you. Besides section headings and subheadings within each chapter, paragraphs are numbered consecutively throughout each chapter for ease of cross-referencing.

If your trip is imminent, see the Time Line Prior to Departure (following the table of contents) to find out what preparations you should make at this stage.

If security is of primary importance to you, the following sections within the indicated chapters specifically cover security issues:

The
Safe Travel
Book

The Safe Travel Book

A Guide for the International Traveler

Peter Savage

Foreword by

James H. Kabler III

Lexington Books

D. C. Heath and Company/Lexington, Massachusetts/Toronto

This book is published as part of the Lexington Books *Issues in Low-Intensity Conflict* series, Neil C. Livingstone, consulting editor.

For information about quantity discounts, contact Lexington Books, D. C. Heath and Company, 125 Spring St., Lexington, MA 02173, 800-235-3565.

Library of Congress Cataloging-in-Publication Data

Savage, Peter
  The safe travel book : a guide for the international traveler / by Peter Savage.
    p. cm.
  ISBN 0-669-17380-0 (alk. paper)
  ISBN 0-669-17381-9 (pbk. : alk. paper)
  1. Travel—Safety measures. I. Title.
G151.S234 1988   910′.2′02—dc19   87-32505

Published simultaneously in Canada
Printed in the United States of America
Casebound International Standard Book Number: 0-669-17380-0
Paperbound International Standard Book Number: 0-669-17381-9
Library of Congress Catalog Card Number 87-32505

The paper used in this publication meets the minimum requirements of American National Standard for Information Sciences—Permanence of Paper for Printed Library Materials, ANSI Z39.48-1984. ♾™

88 89 90 91 92 8 7 6 5 4 3 2 1

Contents

Time Line to Departure Date

The following table indicates which preparations you should be making for your trip, from eight weeks before the trip to your departure date. (Numbers in parentheses refer to paragraph numbers, by chapter, throughout the book.)

Time Before Departure	Routine Measures	Security Measures
8 weeks	Passport photos and application (1.1–1.7) Vaccination requirements— especially cholera and tetanus (1.39–1.43) Visa requirements (1.9–1.15) Order necessary items from mail order catalogues (2.7–2.9, 2.11, 2.12, 2.14–2.16) Call sources of travel, lodging, and security information about basic travel questions (1.87–1.97)	Terrorist contingency planning (1.125–1.127) office and home folders (1.128–1.130)
6 weeks–4 weeks	Air and hotel reservations— make as far in advance as possible, and confirm the week of departure	Review air travel pointers (1.110–1.116) Review hotel reservation security considerations (1.98–1.109)

Time Before Departure	Routine Measures	Security Measures
2 weeks	Start malaria pills (1.78) Passport application—if submitted to Passport Office in person (1.3) International Driver's Permit (1.17) Purchase traveler's checks (1.27–1.30) Review vaccinations, medicines, and health insurance (1.39–1.43, 1.49–1.55, 1.77–1.84) Send advance shipment by courier (2.26)	Review security items on shopping list of essentials (2.11–2.13)
1 week.................	For a last-minute decision to travel, passport application via Congressional Liaison Office (1.5) and visas (1.9) Confirm hotel reservation— note the time and the name of the person contacted	Review security contingency planning (1.125–1.131)
3 days....................	Begin Argonne Anti-Jet-Lag Diet (1.70) Confirm flight reservation Review luggage and apparel (2.19–2.25, 2.27–2.29)	Note emergency contacts (and blood type) on back page of passport and document to be carried in place of passport (1.121, 1.122)
2 days....................	Review what you should carry on your person or have readily accessible in your hand luggage (2.30–2.37)	
1 day	If no advance airline seating reservation, review seating recommendations (3.8–3.10)	Review procedures at the ticket counter (3.1–3.7)
1 day or in-flight...............	Review disembarking procedures (3.21–3.26), procedures from customs to your hotel (4.1–4.11), first steps on arrival at your hotel (4.12–4.25)	

Foreword

This book is a must-read. I underlined so many points in the book that it began to look like a college text. It is vitally important that every American read Peter Savage's book before going overseas.

I was protocol officer at the State Department during the Ford administration and was responsible for over 180 state visits during the Bicentennial. I observed the security precautions that went into these visits and have often reflected since then about how unprotected the average American is when he or she travels abroad.

Today I am president of Nikkal Industries, Ltd., which specializes in the sale of housewares and life-style products worldwide. Nikkal's headquarters are in New York City; there are two overseas subsidiaries, Nikkal Europe (Turino, Italy) and Nikkal Japan (Tokyo). In an average year, I make approximately eight trips to the Far East and four trips to Europe. This year I will begin traveling to South America on a regular basis for the first time.

Although I consider myself an expert traveler, I have picked up innumerable good ideas from this book. *The Safe Travel Book* can make your travel overseas a lot more comfortable. It can also save your life.

I have ordered 100 copies of this book to send to friends and business colleagues because I think it is one of the most important aids to come along in a long time.

—*James H. Kabler III*

Acknowledgments

My heartfelt thanks go to the many people who helped in the preparation of this guide—both in its formative stages and in final review. Some were unaware of the contributions; others knew all too well the demands being made. Thanks to Arna and Gladys, Douglas Ball, George Ball, Kathryn Beckwith, Jean Paul and Mimi Bidegain, Jorge Bustamante, Carlos Campbell, Hanne Caraher, William Colby, Tom Clayton, Worth Daniels, Elizabeth Dax, Kathleen Dickinson, Rich Dumais, C. Burke Elbrick, Frances Harrold, Stephen Jencks, David Jodice, Stan Klinefelter, Robert Kupperman, David Lawson, Helio de Albuquerque Lima, Neil Livingstone, Dorothy Lohmann, Jorge Mester, Jack Ohmans, Jane Otte, Howard Payne, David Phillips, Frank Polk, Barbara Ryan, Tom Reckford, Ina Savage, Serena Savage, Silvine Savage, Ben Sonz, Oscar Sosa, Bryson and Margie Thompson, Jaime Welch-Donahue, and Kim Wheeler.

Introduction

Background and Organization

After breakfast in the hotel café, I sat in the lobby planning my schedule of visits for the day in Bogotá, Colombia. My glance strayed to one entrance just as two gray-haired women labored up the front steps, stood at the head of the stairs, and cried out breathlessly, "We've been robbed!" The hotel staff quickly sat them down, called a policeman (who understood only a few words of English), and vainly tried to contact their tour guide, who was out on a sight-seeing bus on a tour that the ladies had abandoned for a morning of downtown shopping. From their account of what had happened, they were lucky not to have been beaten or stabbed, considering the resistance they gave a band of young assailants in the street. There was no aspect of the incident that could not have been avoided if Arna and her companion, Gladys, had been properly instructed about the dangers they faced on a foreign tour. As a frequent traveler, selling diesel generator sets to industries with specialized electric power needs in Latin America, I was certain that the routine I follow for planning a trip could be reduced to a written formula and put at their disposal.

According to the formula, this travel safety guide is organized to anticipate a traveler's course from the time a trip is planned and a passport applied for to the point of return to the United States. The discussion of each element in this progression is designed to take the mystery out of unfamiliar tasks and to make practical safety precautions part of the planned routine. My thesis is that, rather than being intimidated by unknown hazards, you can enjoy your foreign tour or do your business abroad if you know the risks beforehand and establish a precautionary regimen. (I hope that this guide is in time for Arna's and Gladys's next trip.)

Who Should Read This Guide?

The original draft of this guide was designed to serve inexperienced tourists like Arna and Gladys. Because of increased travel by business sales staff and corporate officers, however, the focus has been widened to cover senior and middle-level executives, who form the largest group of international travelers. The present focus is thus designed to serve first-blush tourists as well as international jet-setters, who will find both a comprehensive plan of action for safe travel and new insights for modifying established security patterns.

The traveler who is being "coached" by this guide—from U.S. passport application to foreign shores and back home—will probably be a business-class traveler accompanied by a working companion or spouse who might never have set foot in a foreign land. The voyage may include side trips to out-of-the-way places as well as trips to major airports and cities.

Nevertheless, the first-class traveler, who expects to be met at the airport by a chauffeured car and to stay only in protected villas, should not ignore the security recommendations given here.

Travelers as Targets

Statistics about Americans in distress abroad, about Americans arrested overseas, and about international terrorism are elusive and imprecise but seem to indicate that conditions have stabilized since a peak of more than 1,000 terrorist incidents in 1979—83 involving American travelers abroad.

Americans in Distress

The U.S. State Department has reported that more than 25,000 U.S. passports are lost or stolen every year and that the number of

Americans left in financial distress or in need of emergency aid from home is increasing (now more than 1,000 per year)—although the department also notes that there is an increasing number of elderly travelers, who have more health problems requiring emergency attention.

Americans Arrested Abroad

The State Department has reported that the arrest rate of Americans abroad is approaching 3,000 annually. About a third are charged with narcotics violations.

Terrorism

The State Department's public reports are not easily interpreted for trends, but the number of "terrorist incidents" involving American citizens seems to have stayed at about 800 per year after the high of about 1,000 per year in the 1979–83 period. The American death toll from terrorism increased to nearly 400 in 1987, but this is difficult to compare with previous statistics (which did not include deaths in certain "war zones"). The death rate could have been spectacularly increased if terrorist bombs on an Air India flight in Canada and an El Al flight in England, both carrying many U.S. citizens, had not been discovered and removed. The terrorist incidents that have occurred seem to indicate that Americans—especially American officials and American Jews—Israelis, and citizens of U.S. allies are the targets of international terrorism, especially since the April 1986 U.S. raids on Libya.

Interpreting the Statistics

These numbers indicate that American travelers should be increasingly alert to the hazards of overseas travel and should prepare for them ahead of time. Compared to the frequency and severity of street crime in most major U.S. cities, however, these statistics show that it is safer to travel abroad than it is to walk down a city street at night in the United States.

Statistics do not account for built-in safeguards that a native of Rio de Janeiro, Paris, New Delhi, or Tokyo programs into a bus ride, a shopping expedition, or a stroll along a major boulevard. For most Americans, safety statistics favor travel over staying at home, but for Arna and Gladys, the percentages were reduced by a lack of informed judgment.

Security specialists agree that there is no such thing as absolute, guaranteed safety from a targeted terrorist attack or a planned criminal activity. Even presidents get shot. They also agree, however, that good planning and routine protective measures can reduce such risk to a minimum. This guide outlines the sensible steps you can take to reduce your exposure and risk without having to go to "Rambo" school.

Cautionary Note

You don't have to follow all the recommendations in this guide to enjoy a safe trip. Many situations are anticipated here that you won't encounter on a week's vacation trip to the Bahamas. However, this is a good checklist, compiled from the experiences of many voyages and from living abroad during times of political upheaval.

Please Send Us Your Comments and Tips

Great effort has been expended to make this as comprehensive a safety guide for travelers as possible. Your comments and suggestions will help make future editions more complete and timely and will help make the world a safer place for travelers. Your comments are welcome; please send them to Peter Savage, Safe Travel Book, c/o Lexington Books, 125 Spring Street, Lexington, MA 02173.

1
Planning Your Trip

Documentation

Passport

1.1 By international convention, a U.S. passport is a document—issued by the U.S. government and addressed to foreign powers—certifying that the person described in the document is a citizen of the United States and requesting permission for the bearer, while abroad, to move freely as well as receive lawful aid and protection. As a mere formal request for permission for the bearer to come and go, a passport is a rather humble document; it definitely does not give Americans rights to U.S. constitutional guarantees or any special treatment under foreign law when they travel. By common practice, a passport is an indispensable traveler registry and control document for foreign security and immigration authorities who stop you at their borders and look for any required entry visas on internal pages and stamp visa pages with your entry and departure dates, a universal identity document for U.S. travelers wishing to register at hotels, make credit card purchases, buy local currency or rent a car, and, perhaps most importantly, a guarantee for you and a notice to foreign authorities that the U.S. Embassy has an interest if you are in trouble. Because of this guarantee of official U.S. interest, it is often a useful document to carry even in countries which do not require a passport to travel, such as Canada. Obtaining a passport is your first step in preparing to travel abroad.

1.2 Obtaining a passport is not complicated, but it can be a tedious bureaucratic exercise. The requirements discussed in the following paragraphs are listed in Bureau of Consular Affairs, *Your Trip Abroad,* Department of State Publication 8872, available from the **U.S. Department of State,** Washington, DC 20520, or at U.S. Passport Offices.

1.3 To obtain a new passport, you will need the following documentation:

- Proof of U.S. citizenship, shown by:
  —A certified copy of your birth certificate (Passport Offices ask that the certification have a raised seal, not just an ink stamp) or
  —A previously issued passport (within eight years of expiration, you may apply for a renewal rather than a new passport)
  —If you were born abroad, a naturalization certificate or a statement from the clerk of the court of naturalization stating that you were naturalized in the court on a stated date
- Two identical front-view photos (2″ × 2″) which may be two copies of a home photo but which must have a light background and be in clear focus (the best procedure is to get six or eight passport photos at one sitting so that you can carry extras for other documents, such as an international driver's license, or to replace a stolen passport abroad)
- A completed passport application form (Form DSP-11), available at any U.S. Passport Office and most central post offices.

The passport application form ends with a statement affirming that all the information you have provided is true and accurate, so you must sign the form in the presence of the post office employee who attends to passport applications, the clerk of a court, or an officer of the U.S. Passport Office. It is important that you sign this application exactly as you wish your name to appear on your passport, even if this is not your full name as it appears on your birth certificate or as you sign your checks. There may be good safety reasons to use your first initial instead of your first name or to omit your first name altogether (see 1.5, point 5, p. 4).

Note: When you present the application form, you will be required to show independent identification, such as a driver's license, an existing passport, or other documentation that includes your photograph.

All of this documentation will be sealed at the post office and mailed to the U.S. Passport Office for processing and return by mail (in several weeks to two months) with your new passport. You may hasten this process by taking the application and supporting documentation directly to a Passport Office.

1.4 To obtain a passport renewal (which may be done by mail), you will need the following documentation:

- A valid U.S. passport close to its expiration date (usually within six months) so that a new one is necessary, or an expired passport less than eight years from its expiration date (if more than eight years, you must apply for a *new* passport)
- Two passport photos (same as for a new passport)
- A completed renewal passport application form (Form DSP-82, Application for Passport by Mail). As for a new passport, sign the renewal form just as you wish your name to appear on your new passport, even if it is different from the way it appears on the old passport (see 1.5 for safety reasons for doing this)
- A check or money order for $35 (do not send cash by mail)

You may put everything in an envelope and send it directly to any U.S. Passport Office or take it to your local post office, where it will be sealed and mailed to the Passport Office. Again, expect a wait of six weeks to two months for the return of your passport.

1.5 You should consider the following points when you are applying for a passport:

- Allow at least six weeks to receive your passport if you apply for it by mail. If you go directly to the Passport Office with the required documentation, allow one to two weeks. Add time for getting necessary visas (see 1.9).
- If you expect to use the passport extensively, request a passport with extra pages (up to forty-eight).

- If delays are likely, call the office of your representative in Congress and ask them to recommend you to the Congressional Liaison Office, which usually takes one week to produce a passport if your application and photos are in order. In an emergency, a passport can be issued in a single day (see also 1.7).
- If further delays are likely (for example, in a season when there is a large backlog), call other Passport Offices to find out whether their processing time is faster. (Passport Offices are located in Boston, Chicago, Honolulu, Houston, Los Angeles, Miami, New Orleans, New York, Philadelphia, San Francisco, Seattle, Stamford [CT], and Washington, D.C.)
- If you already have a valid passport, make sure that old entry stamps will not be a problem in your country of destination this time (for example, Israeli entry stamps when you are bound for some Arab states). If they might be a problem, get a new passport.
- If you carry an Official Passport or a Diplomatic Passport, also get a tourist passport for you and for each member of your family. This will be useful for traveling to countries where you are not accredited and will keep you and members of your family as removed as possible from U.S. officialdom in case of a terrorist incident.
- Although your legal surname must appear on your passport, you may wish to abbreviate some given names if you have several. For convenience, for example, if you never use your first name, put your first initial and middle name (the name you *do* use) on your passport so that someone who pages you at an airport according to the name on your passport will call a name you will recognize. There is also a security reason for using an initial instead of a given name if the given name might draw the unfavorable attention of a terrorist (for example, Saul Edward Stone would be given as S. Edward Stone).
- Get several extra copies of your passport photo (always in multiples of 2) to use on visas, driver's permits, local permits abroad, and items such as tennis club cards—or for a new passport if yours is lost or stolen.

1.6 Address further questions regarding passports to **Washington Passport Agency,** 1425 K Street, N.W., Washington, DC 20524. The phone number for a recorded message is (202)783-8200; for public inquiries, call (202)523-1355. If this line is busy and you are in a hurry, try calling the Passport Office in New York, New Orleans, or another city.

1.7 Passport and visa services are available from travel service companies and large travel agencies. One such service company is **Travisa,** 2121 P Street, N.W., Washington, DC 10037; 1-800-222-2589. Another service company is **Passport Plus,** based in New York (1-800-367-1818). Letting the travel agency or service company do the legwork and the waiting in line can save you much time and aggravation (and can get you a passport within four working days if all your documents are in order, within one day if you can show by the date on your airline ticket that travel is imminent).

1.8 Cautionary notes regarding when and where to carry your passport are provided in:

2.30 What You Should Carry on Your Person or Have Readily Accessible in Your Hand Luggage;
3.20 What to Do During a Terrorist Hijacking;
5.5. Don't Carry Your Passport Unless You Need It.

Visas

1.9 Call the consular section of the embassy of each destination country to find out whether a visa or health documentation is required and to ask about required documentation and processing time. Also inquire about exit requirements. Your questions should cover all of the following points:

- Visa requirements and processing time
- Immunization and health document requirements for entry to or passage through the country
- Exit requirements

- Documentation requirements for minor children traveling with one parent (or alone)
- Currency restrictions:
  —Allowed to enter with U.S. dollars?
  —Allowed to enter with local currency?
  —Allowed to exchange dollars for local currency freely, or only at central bank offices?
  —Other currency restrictions (for example, exit restrictions)?
- Medical certificates required for any prescription drugs you plan to carry
- Public health services available in an emergency (specifically, is treatment free or must you pay for it or have insurance?)
- Licensing, permit, and insurance requirements for any vehicle to be driven or taken there or for your driving a vehicle there
- Items that may not be taken into the country
- Internal travel restrictions and permits (for example, for various security reasons, Peru, India, Nicaragua and many communist countries have internal travel restrictions and unpredictable return passage from various points within the country).

1.10 If you plan to visit a country only once or twice, a tourist visa is probably all that is necessary. If you will be making many repeated visits, you should probably request a business or other visa that allows frequent entry.

Note: Before applying for visas, consider how repeated entries to any country are going to be explained to local authorities on reentry. A tourist visa may serve for two or three business trips, but repeated trips may draw the attention of immigration officials, and you might not be permitted to leave the country without showing either that you have not earned taxable income or that you have registered with tax authorities. To save time and avoid contrived explanations later, it may prove more practical to get a business visa in the first place. One alternative is to get a new passport after several visits; past entry stamps will not appear in the new document. At the border, the most expeditious and best understood explanation of your visit is "pleasure trips." Strive to have your documents consistent with that explanation.

1.11 Business visas can be inconvenient in some cases. Many countries, such as Venezuela, require income tax clearance or payment on income before departure, which may require advance application. Also, no processing is done on weekends and holidays.

1.12 Get a visa with the longest validity period possible, so that you may not have to get a new visa on your next visit. France, for example, now issues three-month and eighteen-month visas; the eighteen-month visa is slightly more expensive.

1.13 Worldwide visa requirements are listed on the *World Status Map,* issued monthly ($4.50/month) by World Status Map, Box 466, Merrifield, VA 22116; 1-301-564-8473. It also provides Department of State traveler's advisories and immunization information.

1.14 If you are traveling with a child, documented permission from the parents (or the other parent) may be required. Such requirements are most stringent in Latin American countries (for example, Mexico), where a single parent, especially a woman, may have to present translated, certified divorce papers or the death certificate of the other parent to justify custody of a minor. (In Argentina the father's written, notarized consent is required for a minor to travel alone or with the mother.)

1.15 Once your passport and visas have been prepared, make two photocopies of all passport and visa pages—one copy to carry separately in case your passport is lost or stolen, one copy to leave in your office or home folder (see 1.129 and 1.130).

Vehicle and Driver's Permits

1.16 If you take a vehicle with you or you are driving across an international border (for example, to Mexico), you may need a temporary vehicle import permit. You should also find out whether your liability insurance is valid in the foreign country (for example, liability, collision, and comprehensive coverage insurance issued by U.S. companies is not valid in Mexico).

1.17 The International Driver's Permit and the Inter-American Driver's Permit are permits to drive that are based on a valid U.S. driver's license—they are *not* driver's licenses in themselves. They are often unnecessary except in countries that require that any license have an authorized translation into the local language (for example, Japan) where the permit is a recognized translation. Some countries (for example, Mexico and Bermuda) do not recognize U.S. driver's licenses but do recognize the international permits.

The International Driver's permit, which is valid for one year, can be obtained by AAA members at any central AAA office for $15. The permit, which requires two passport photos, can be prepared during your visit to the AAA office.

1.18 There are several good reasons to get an international permit:

- The International Driver's Permit and the Inter-American Driver's Permit entitle bearers to reciprocal motor club services abroad (that is, travel information maps, emergency road service and towing, insurance)
- The International Driver's Permit, through its AAA affiliation, entitles its holders to discounts through the Alliance of International Tourism (based in Geneva, Switzerland) on various service trips, and hotels
- Both permits are recognized by international conventions as identity documents and can be carried locally—*not for crossing international borders*—in place of a passport when the passport has been lost or stolen

A central AAA office can tell you by phone which countries offer full auto club reciprocity or limited reciprocity.

Note: In less developed countries, this document can often be extremely useful in negotiations with local police, who may never have seen such a document. Therefore, their inquiries tend to focus on the official-looking document itself, rather than on your traffic transgressions.

Credit Cards and Financial Documentation

1.19 The American Express Card is useful because of its cash availability features (up to $2,000 with a Gold credit card in U.S.-dollar traveler's checks—*not* cash or local currency).

Other American Express Card benefits include $100,000 automatic flight life insurance and $500 baggage insurance. On request, Gold card holders can have $500,000 life insurance for a $5.50 charge. Other Gold cards, including VISA, have comparable features.

Note: Many small establishments do not accept American Express but prefer Diner's Club, VISA, or MasterCard. This is especially true throughout Latin America and in small shops in Europe.

1.20 If you will need check-cashing privileges, regional banks in the United States can recommend you to a correspondent bank or can draw a traveler's letter of credit for presentation to the correspondent bank. There is usually a 1 to 3 percent charge for such a letter of credit. Because of the cash availability features of credit cards, however, many banks no longer offer travelers' letters of credit.

1.21 Make a list of all your credit card numbers or photocopy all your credit cards on a single page; leave one copy at your office or home and carry a second copy with you—separate from your credit cards—for reference in case you lose the cards (see 1.129 and 1.130).

Note: All credit card companies calculate foreign exchange at the time they process your bill—not at the time of the transaction, when you use the card. Don't overspend your credit card limit in stores abroad. Foreign vendors do not take mistakes lightly and may call local police if they check with your credit card company, find your limit overspent, and risk nonpayment for your purchases (see also 6.6, Pros and Cons of Using Cash or Credit Cards).

1.22   If you lose your credit cards, call the following numbers:

- American Express: 1-800-327-2177
- VISA: Call collect to the United States—(703)827-8400; or, in Europe, call London 973-8111; if you have a Premier Card, call (415)570-3200
- MasterCard: Call collect to the United States—(314)275-6100; or, in the United States, call 1-800-826-2181.
- Diner's Club (and Carte Blanche): 1-800-525-9135

Exchanging Currency Before You Travel

1.23   To avoid delays after your arrival abroad, you may wish to buy enough foreign currency before you leave to cover the cost of transportation from the airport to your hotel and tips to bellhops and the like. You are likely to get the *least* favorable exchange rate at U.S. banks and U.S. airports of embarkation. Thus, you should purchase only what you need for immediate expenses on arrival. Another problem with advance purchase of foreign currency is that U.S. dealers have only large denomination bills—not the small change you are looking for.

Note: In times of currency exchange fluctuations and harsh overseas exchange rate controls, there may be good reason to stock up on foreign currencies before leaving the United States. In such times, you should heed the answers to the following questions with great care and act on the advice.

1.24   A good travel agent should be able to tell you what you need to know about foreign exchange:

- How much to buy in advance
- Where to obtain the most favorable rate (usually at a bank— rarely at a hotel)
- Whether there is a significant increase in rate if actual dollars are exchanged (as opposed to traveler's checks or personal checks)
- Consequences of illegal exchange

- Necessity (and advisability) of registering foreign currency on entry
- The dos and don'ts of black market purchases
- Exit restrictions on foreign currency

1.25 If your travel agent cannot help or says that it is not a problem (a certain sign that it *is* a problem), call the international division of a U.S. bank that does business in your country of destination and ask to speak to an officer who handles loans there.

Deak-Perera, the foreign exchange house, is also a good source of information, although they are less likely to be forthcoming with information about black market rates or reasons to exchange money after you arrive abroad.

1.26 It may be useful to carry from $50 to $100 in U.S. one-dollar or five-dollar bills so that you can pay initial cab fares and porters' tips in small denominations of U.S. currency (and avoid giving unintended lavish tips in an unknown currency). This procedure avoids the need for exchanging currency until you are in your hotel or until your overseas customer/client/host can give you guidance. However, such payments in U.S. currency are illegal in some countries (for example, Jamaica, Nicaragua, and most communist countries), so check beforehand (see also 4.3).

Traveler's Checks

1.27 Traveler's checks are useful because they are safe (you can get your money back if they are lost) and commonly accepted, but they may not solve the problem of an immediate need for small amounts of foreign currency. American Express, for example, no longer issues checks in denominations smaller than $20—usually too much for your cab ride from the airport.

1.28 If you have any influence whatsoever at institutions that issue traveler's checks, you should be able to purchase them without a fee. For example, if you are a member of AAA, you can purchase all major traveler's checks without a fee up to the limit of your credit on any major credit card.

1.29   You should also find out which traveler's checks are the best known and most accepted in the country of destination (American Express, Citibank, Bank of America, Barclay's Bank, VISA, Thomas Cook, and so on).

1.30   In a fast-changing currency exchange market, it may be better to buy traveler's checks in French francs, British pounds, German deutsche marks or Japanese yen, rather than in dollars. Foreign-currency traveler's checks are available in the currencies of Australia, Canada, Holland, England, France, Germany, Hong Kong, Japan, Switzerland, and the United States.

1.31   Keep good records of your traveler's check numbers if you want efficient recovery for lost or stolen traveler's checks. Obviously, these records should be kept apart from the checks themselves, or the list will also be lost or stolen. A list of your traveler's check numbers should also be kept in your office or home travel folder (see 1.129 and 1.130).

1.32   American Express will replace U.S.-dollar traveler's checks in the amount lost within twenty-four hours. This can be done, however, only at an American Express travel office and usually only during normal business hours. In some countries in Europe and Latin America, American Express has special provisions for emergencies whereby Avis agencies can replace lost checks with cash in local currency—but this requires a collect call to American Express in the United States (see 1.33 for the number to call).

   Thomas Cook traveler's checks, provided without a fee by most travel agents and some banks, has an emergency replacement arrangement with Hertz for up to $250 when agencies and banks aren't open.

   Replacement of VISA traveler's checks requires that you locate a bank that handles them during business hours or that you call collect to the United States (see 1.33); an operator is on duty around the clock to direct you to a local agent who handles emergencies.

   Citibank and Bank of America traveler's checks can be replaced at banks or branch offices that handle them, but only during business hours.

1.33   To replace lost traveler's checks, call collect to the following telephone numbers in the United States from abroad:

- American Express: (801)968-8300
- Thomas Cook: (212)974-5696
- VISA: (415)574-7111
- MasterCard: (212)974-5700
- Citibank: (813)879-7701
- Bank of America: (415)622-3800

Personal Checks

1.34   Don't rely on being able to cash personal checks abroad. It is often difficult to cash personal checks overseas, where your credit and the collectibility of your check are unknown to the payee. A letter of reference or credit from your U.S. bank to its correspondent bank or the assistance of your customer/client/host at his or her bank *may* facilitate cashing checks abroad.

1.35   As a matter of personal security, you should carry your personal checks separate from documents that show your signature (such as your passport and traveler's checks). Also don't carry them with a check register or stubs that show large cash balances or deposits to your account. If you must carry such records with your checks, review them before you travel as if each entry would have to be explained to a terrorist hijacker (see also 2.6).

Immunizations, Medicines, and Health

1.36   This section has been reviewed by several doctors and though some disagree with specific recommendations, they agree unanimously with some general precautions: (1) avoid taking any medicines unless they are specifically indicated; (2) avoid taking prescription drugs unless you are advised to do so by a doctor; and (3) if you have a health condition that may require treatment, expect to have to treat it while you are traveling. Under most circumstances, it may be prudent to anticipate your need for prescription drugs and carry them with you. However, don't use them unless you are treating the illness for which they were prescribed or until a doctor tells you to use them.

Advance planning for dealing with illness and disability may be more than a matter of carrying prescription drugs. If you have a pin in your hip or are extremely out of shape, expect to have to walk much more when you travel than you do at home. Expect to find no crutches or wheelchairs, even at airports, and plan on finding only steps, no ramps, at airports and public places. If you have a bad back, expect it to go out. Count on seats that force you to slouch and on beds that are too soft. It is axiomatic that anything that *can* go wrong, *will* go wrong (usually on a Sunday afternoon) when you travel.

Leave a list of any unusual health conditions and/or medicinal restrictions in your office or home folder during your trip (see 1.129 and 1.130).

Your Medical Records

1.37 Your personal physician should have a guide showing any immunizations or medicines that might be required in your country of destination. Your physician should also have records of your past innoculations for reference.

1.38 An International Certificate of Vaccinations from the World Health Organization, with records of your past immunizations, is a valuable document to have with you if you become sick abroad. It will tell a local doctor your current immunization status, and it will also serve as proof to local authorities that you have had the yellow fever or cholera immunizations that may be required for entering a country or even for just transiting it to go elsewhere. Having this certificate may save you from on-the-spot vaccination, denied entry, or quarantine. Also file a copy of the certificate or other immunization record in your home or office folder (see 1.129 and 1.130).

An International Certificate of Vaccination is available from the U.S. Government Printing Office, stock no. 017-001-00-440-5, at 8660 Cherry Lane, Laurel, MD 20707-4980 for $2, (301)792-0262 or (202)275-2091 and may be filled in by the physician administering the vaccinations, except for yellow fever, which is administered at certain clinics so that batch numbers of the vaccination can be controlled. (See also 1.80, Other Medical Precautions.)

Guides to Medicines or Shots You May Need

1.39 The World Status Map lists on a monthly updated basis what countries require cholera and yellow fever vaccination, as well as listing new visa requirements and State Department Traveler's Advisories. It is available through World Status Map, Box 466, Merrifield, VA 22116, (301)564-8473. The cost is $4.50 per month.

1.40 The Georgetown University School of Medicine, International Health Service (Department of Community and Family Medicine), Washington, DC 20007, provides information by telephone on vaccinations that are required worldwide. Call (202)625-7379 or (202)625-6574.

Note: These office telephone lines are supposed to be answered from 8:30 to 5:00 on business days, but they are often busy or do not answer at all. Also, a person who is able to answer your questions may be available only at certain hours.

The Georgetown University International Health Service also issues papers to the public entitled "What You Should Know About Malaria" and "What You Should Know About Traveler's Diarrhea."

1.41 Johns Hopkins University, The International Health Clinic, Hampton House, Room 113, 624 North Broadway, Baltimore, MD 21205, offers a complete range of vaccines, accompanied by pretrip and posttrip consultations with doctors who specialize in infectious diseases and international health. Call (301)955-8931 weekdays from 9:00 to 5:00.

1.42 Outside the Washington, D.C., area, call your state health department to find out which local clinic can give you information about immunizations and administer yellow fever shots if they are required.

1.43 *Health Information for International Travel,* (HHS Publication CDC 81-8280) is available from the U.S. Government Printing Office, Washington, DC 20402 for about $5. It is published annually by the Public Health Service, Centers for Disease Control (Atlanta, GA 30333) and specifies what vaccinations are required by different countries and includes much detailed information on measures for travelers to take to protect their health and facilitate their travel. It includes maps showing areas of special risk for malaria and yellow fever as well as a description and recommendation about a series of common overseas diseases.

Medical Assistance Abroad

1.44 The International Association for Medical Assistance to Travellers (IAMAT), 736 Center Street, Lewiston, NY 14092, (716)754-4883, issues a free, regularly updated membership booklet listing health institutions and doctors worldwide (with phone numbers). A stated purpose of the IAMAT is to match travelers in need of medical help with doctors who can speak the language of the patient. IAMAT also provides updated guides to health problems related to food and climate as well as to such maladies as malaria and schistosomiasis. Publications are free, with an expected donation to IAMAT.

1.45 U.S. embassies can provide names of doctors to be contacted in emergencies. For the most part, these doctors can speak English, but they are not necessarily otherwise qualified to serve your medical needs (see also 5.63).

1.46 If you are staying at a large hotel, the hotel desk will usually be able to find you a doctor in an emergency, even on weekends. There is no assurance that such a doctor will speak English or will in any other way be qualified to help you, but he or she will probably be familiar with maladies normally suffered by visiting travelers.

1.47 The best source of information about reliable medical assistance abroad may be your own doctor, who might be able to recommend a doctor in your country of destination, or your customer/client/host, who should be able to recommend a local doctor or clinic.

1.48   If you receive medical treatment abroad, get a written report from the doctor or institution that can be reviewed and understood by your doctor back home.

Health Insurance and Emergency Referral Plans

1.49   As of this writing, world health care seems to be a burgeoning business; insurance groups, established health organizations, and international traveler organizations regularly announce new referral and direct aid plans. Some new and established plans are discussed here, but some that were listed in travel guides as recently as 1986 are no longer in service. It would be best to discuss any plan that interests you with an insurance broker or agent who handles policies of well-known companies. At the very least, determine which insurer stands behind the plan, how long the plan has been in business, and what its source is for the list of recommended doctors or medical providers. Some of the new life and health insurance plans also cover security advice, terrorist hijackings, risk management, and ransom negotiation, as well as medical or death benefits. Such plans should also be reviewed by a responsible insurance broker or agent.

1.50   American Express has a new referral service, Global Assist, for when you need medical or legal assistance overseas. Subscribers are given an around-the-clock telephone number to call to receive the name and means of contacting an English-speaking specialist to suit their needs. Global Assist is exclusively a referral plan, not an insurance plan. Information on the plan is available by calling American Express National Marketing Department in New York, 1-800-528-4800 (in the Washington, D.C., area, 1-800-554-2639).

1.51   A new insurance plan is available from Travel Assistance International (TAI) Inc., 1333 F Street, N.W., Suite 300, Washington, DC 20004, 1-800-821-2828. This is an individual traveler's health insurance plan, not including emergency evacuation, with coverage limited to $5,000. For coverage of groups of ten or more regular travelers, however, TAI has an unlimited emergency care and evacuation insurance program as well as a reimbursable complete assistance plan to cover items not covered by your present insurer. TAI service is based on a network of medical contacts built up by Europ Assistance Worldwide, Inc., Paris, France, which was started by a group of European insurance companies in 1971.

Note: Emergency evacuation of a patient from a medical facility that may not screen donor blood for antibodies to the AIDS virus in a high-risk area *may* be justified by the TAI group plan if local and TAI specialists agree.

1.52 A new insurance plan was announced in 1986 by Access America—a subsidiary of Blue Cross and Blue Shield of Washington, D.C. For details of Access America, which covers a wide range of medical assistance and other travel-related services, call 1-800-851-2800. This plan does cover emergency evacuation for individual travelers, including evacuation where there is a risk of receiving blood unscreened for AIDS, but coverage is limited to $10,000. This plan is also offered as Trip Assist International by AAA (same toll-free number).

1.53 Health Care Abroad, International Underwriter/Brokers, Inc., 1029 Investment Building, 1511 K Street, N.W., Washington, DC 20005, 1-800-336-3310, provides comprehensive sickness, accident, and major medical coverage. A medical evacuation plan for locations where blood is not screened for AIDS is available.

1.54 International SOS, Assistance, One Neshaming Interplex, Trevose, PA 19047, 1-800-323-8930 or (215)244-1500, has a medical service program with a round-the-clock telephone referral to a network of medical centers. SOS, which has been in business for over a decade, also provides pretravel emergency planning and standby alert services for major international firms.

Note: The International Airline Passengers Association (IAPA) has recently announced an insurance program that provides a comprehensive security package—security advice, risk management, ransom negotiation—as well as medical and death benefits. The cost of the insurance is $200 to $300 per year in addition to the basic membership fee of $90. Information about the IAPA Control Risks Programme and other IAPA services is available by writing Box 660074, Dallas, TX 75266-0074, (214)520-1070 or 1-800-527-5888. Control Risk Limited, the international security consulting firm participating in the IAPA program (a London-based firm with ties to Lloyds of London insurance underwriters) has established a position as one of several responsible security advisory, investigation, and negotiation firms over the last ten years. Control Risk may be contacted directly in the United States at 4350 East-West Highway, Suite 900, Bethesda, MD 20814, (301)654-2075.

1.55 Your present insurance plan may already provide adequate coverage overseas. Furthermore, if you plan to travel to England, Canada, the Soviet Union and many other countries where medical treatment is a free state service, you may not need insurance. You should review your present insurance coverage to see that it dovetails with any new coverage you may require.

AIDS (Acquired Immune Deficiency Syndrome)

1.56 Only a foolhardy traveler with suicidal tendencies would seek out liaisons that might bear the risk of AIDS. The greatest risk to the traveler thus comes from an emergency blood transfusion at a hospital or clinic in a country where AIDS is endemic and where donor blood is not screened for the antibody to the virus that causes AIDS. In such clinics, improperly sterilized needles may also constitute a risk (see 2.10).

1.57 A company plan of action must be devised whereby representatives traveling in high-risk countries and requiring a blood transfusion will be taken to safe health facilities where blood screened for AIDS is available. Such a plan, which should provide for emergency evacuation, should also be included in your office or home travel files (see 1.129 and 1.130).

Note: The Access America insurance plan covers such emergency evacuation (but limits all coverage to a $10,000 ceiling) and the Travel Assistance International, Inc., group plans cover such evacuation without any limitation, provided that specialists for TAI agree that such evacuation is warranted. Other plans also cover emergency evacuation where there is a risk of AIDS-contaminated transfusions (see 1.50–1.54).

1.58 The countries where there are reports of increased cases of AIDS (as of September 1987) and where there is likely to be a risk that blood used for transfusions has not been screened for AIDS are as follows:

- In the Americas: Brazil, Haiti, Mexico
- In Africa: Burundi, Kenya, Malawi, Rwanda, Tanzania, Uganda, Zaire, Zambia

(*Source:* Thomas C. Quinn, M.D., "The International Impact of AIDS," September 1986, paper available from the Johns Hopkins University, The International Health Clinic, Hampton House, 624 North Broadway, Baltimore, MD 21205)
    Updated information is available from the Department of Health and Human Services, Public Health Service, Centers for Disease Control, Atlanta, GA 30333, (404)329-3472.

Travelers' Diarrhea (TD)

1.59 The diet you plan to follow (or to abandon) during your trip abroad may determine what medicines you should carry or have prescribed. If your tour will include a rich gourmet dinner with several different kinds of wine every night, and if this is a change from your routine at home, you should expect an upset stomach and drowsiness during your trip. If your tour will also include a tight schedule of sight-seeing visits to archeological ruins in the summer sun, dehydration should be a concern, and you should have a safe source of bottled water or Coca-Cola. Beer is safe but may make you drowsy. It would be wise to consult with your doctor before you start your trip.

Finding remedies once you are abroad and afflicted can be chancy. Pharmacists in most foreign countries have a much broader license to diagnose symptoms and prescribe drugs than American druggists do. However, although they often are familiar with local maladies and with what works to cure them, they don't know your medical history. Also, they have access to drugs that have not met the tests of those sold over the counter in the United States. Some guidelines for what you may take for traveler's diarrhea or food poisoning—which may be a serious problem—are included in the following paragraphs. Recommendations are from the National Institutes of Health (NIH) publication, *Consensus Development Conference Statement on Travelers' Diarrhea,* January 1985 (hereafter referred to as the NIH Statement).

1.60 Travelers' diarrhea (TD) is caused by food and/or water contaminated by both bacteria and viruses from feces. It often comes from raw vegetables, raw meat, raw seafood, drinking water, ice, unpasteurized milk, dairy products, and unpeeled fruits.

Note: The International Health Service at Georgetown University (as well as many seasoned travelers) says that even slight changes of diet in a new environment will produce mild diarrhea and that treatment should be avoided until after your system has been purged of the food that produced the initial symptoms. Treat only persistent or recurring diarrhea.

1.61 TD can be prevented by meticulous attention to what you eat (and its preparation) and drink, especially water. Do not use tap water to drink, to brush your teeth, or for ice in drinks. Drink only bottled water or bottled liquids. Coke and beer are safe standbys. Order bottled water for use in your hotel room. When you get bottled water, check the seal or cap to see that it has not been opened, and watch the attendant remove the cap in your presence. For rustic areas, carry water purification tablets.

1.62 The NIH Statement recommends against taking any preventive agents before traveling (although some data have shown that active ingredients in Pepto-Bismol, Bactrim, and Septra do decrease chances of getting diarrhea, whereas Lomotil has not been found to be an effective preventive agent). Because of side effects—and depending on the area of risk—the NIH Statement recommends medical consultation prior to preventive use.

1.63 The following medicines are often suggested for less severe, nonmicrobial TD. Generic names of active ingredients, for use abroad where the medicines might not be known by their brand names, are given in parentheses:

- Pepto-Bismol (bismuth subsalicylate): reduces bowel symptoms, does not require a prescription, slower acting than medicines listed below, which require a prescription in the United States, (may be dangerous for people with kidney problems or those who take aspirin for other ailments)
- Lomotil (diphenoxylate)   opium derivatives that reduce
- Imodium (loperamide)   bowel symptoms, require a pre-
- Paregoric   scription in the United States
- Codeine   (don't use for patients with high fever and blood in bowel movements; also, discontinue if symptoms persist beyond forty-eight hours)
- Kaopectate (kaolin and pectin): gives bowel movements more consistency, does not reduce other symptoms, does not require a prescription
- Activated charcoal: ineffective, does not reduce symptoms

1.64 The following medicines have been recommended for severe, microbial TD (attended by three or more loose bowel movements per eight-hour period, nausea, vomiting, cramps, fever, blood in stools):

- Bactrim or Septra (trimethoprim/   antibiotic drugs, reduces sulfamethoxazole, or TMP/SMX)   duration and severity of
- Vibramycin (doxycycline)   symptoms

Note: If TD remains severe for more than thirty-six hours after starting antibiotics, medical attention should be sought urgently.

Note: Nausea and vomiting without diarrhea should *not* be treated with antibiotic drugs listed above.

1.65 Although TD does not necessarily result in dehydration, fluid and electrolyte balance can be maintained by drinking potable fruit juices and soft drinks and eating salted crackers. The International Health Service of Georgetown University School of Medicine (see 1.40) recommends curing fluid and electrolyte deficiency after TD by drinking: (1) an 8-ounce glass of orange, apple, or other fruit juice, adding one-half teaspoon of honey or corn syrup and one pinch of table salt, and (2) an 8-ounce glass of potable water, adding one-quarter teaspoon of baking soda.

Fatigue

1.66 Most seasoned travelers agree that foreign travel by means of any public carrier is hard work and invariably involves elements of unpredictability. For this reason, it is best to be well rested, in good health, and in a sound frame of mind when you start a business or pleasure trip. Being in good physical and mental health is also an important personal security consideration. Being alert to possible danger and attentive to what is going on around you after you have been traveling requires a measure of endurance. Thus, being healthy increases your chances of staying safe and surviving any crisis.

1.67 Use luggage that has shoulder straps or handles that do not dig into your hands. Use a portable, wheeled bag carrier for heavy luggage. Practice hefting your luggage prior to travel. Be sure to bend your legs to pick up heavy luggage; do not bend over, using your back. Most travelers are unaccustomed to being beasts of burden, so expect aches and pains, and learn to pace yourself (see also 2.19, Luggage).

1.68 Plan to travel in shoes that are serviceable and comfortable. Never travel in new shoes or in boots that are difficult to get off and on in a confined area, such as an airplane seat.

1.69 Dress for comfort and ease of movement, especially for air travel. In the tourist or business section of a jumbo jet, you are going to be herded like cows, so do not dress your best. Fancy dressers are also likely to catch the eye of pickpockets and terrorist hijackers (see also 2.24 and 2.25, Clothing).

Jet Lag

1.70 The jet lag cure with the best reputation to date is the Argonne National Laboratory Anti-Jet-Lag diet. This diet starts three days before departure and alternates between feast and fast days. You can get complete instructions (as shown in Figure 1–1) free on a small, wallet-sized card by sending a self-addressed, stamped envelope to The Anti-Jet-Lag Diet, Argonne National Laboratory, Argonne, IL 60439, (312)972-5575.

1.71 With the press of last-minute business before departure, observing an unusual routine for meals is often unmanageable. Therefore, a diet like the Argonne Lab diet is difficult to maintain. Also, airline meals are not usually arranged according to the formula. One alternative used by some business travelers for short stays in different time zones is to maintain their home working hours—starting early (or late) and leaving the office early (or late), according to their accustomed time in the United States. Similarly, for stays of longer duration, these travelers shift gradually from their home working hours to the local schedule, changing by a few hours every day over the course of a week.

1.72 One major component of "jet lag effect" is exhaustion, caused by the continuous, mild (sometimes not so mild) motion and buffeting of the airplane, air pressure changes, and the tension of facing unexpected events. Travelers going from north to south, with only a small time change, should also expect to experience jet lag symptoms, no matter what their diet.

1.73 Health specialists and frequent travelers consistently advise that you sleep on the plane (take a sleeping tablet, if necessary), stay awake on arrival and work during daylight hours if you can, avoid alcoholic beverages in flight and on arrival, and avoid stimulants such as coffee to overcome drowsiness until your system has adapted to the change in schedule.

1.74 Recent research is trying to identify drugs that can bring a traveler's circadian (bio) rhythm into phase with a new daytime /nighttime environment. The focus of the research is on the effects of the hormone melatonin on the sleep/waking cycle. Although experimentation and testing are still in progress, several medical experts involved in the project claim that melatonin is successful in overcoming the effects of jet lag.

Medicines to Carry with You

1.75 The following are basic medicinal items you should have with you (see also 2.10, which lists both medicinal and nonmedicinal medical items):

- Aspirin or your preferred substitute (such as Tylenol) and stronger pain-killers as recommended by your doctor (particularly for pains caused by walking long distances and carrying heavy luggage)
- Medicine for diarrhea:
  —For milder, nonmicrobial diarrhea (see 1.63): Pepto-Bismol (decreases rate of stooling), which comes in tablet form; Lomotil, Imodium (capsules), paregoric, or codeine (antimotility agents that reduce symptoms, provide temporary relief), which all require a prescription;
  —For severe, microbial diarrhea, attended by three or more loose stools in eight hours, nausea, vomiting, cramps, fever, blood in stools (see 1.64): Bactrim, Septra, or Vibramycin (antibiotic agents that reduce severity and duration of symptoms) which are antibiotics that require a prescription
- Antacid (like TUMS) to counter effects of unfamiliar foreign food
- Band-Aids and Bacitracin (antiseptic ointment) to protect open cuts or blisters
- Cold remedy pills

How to avoid jet lag:

1. **DETERMINE BREAKFAST TIME** at destination on day of arrival.

2. **FEAST-FAST-FEAST-FAST** on home time. Start three days before departure day. On day one, FEAST; eat heartily with high-protein breakfast and lunch and a high-carbohydrate dinner. No coffee except between 3 and 5 p.m. On day two, FAST on light meals of salads, light soups, fruits and juices. Again, no coffee except between 3 and 5 p.m. On day three, FEAST again. On day four, departure day, FAST; if you drink caffeinated beverages, take them in morning when traveling west, or between 6 and 11 p.m. when traveling east. Going west, you may fast only half day.

3. **BREAK FINAL FAST** at destination breakfast time. No alcohol on plane. If flight is long enough, sleep until normal breakfast time at destination, *but no later*. Wake up and FEAST on high-protein breakfast. Stay awake, active. Continue day's meals according to meal times at destination.

FEAST on high protein breakfasts and lunches to stimulate the body's active cycle. Suitable meals include steak, eggs, hamburgers, high-protein cereals, green beans.

FEAST on high-carbohydrate suppers to stimulate sleep. They include spaghetti and other pastas (but no meatballs), crepes (but no meat filling), potatoes, other starchy vegetables, and sweet desserts.

FAST days help deplete the liver's store of carbohydrates and prepare the body's clock for resetting. Suitable foods include fruit, light soups, broths, skimpy salads, unbuttered toast, half pieces of bread. Keep calories and carbohydrates to a minimum.

Figure 1–1. *The Argonne National Laboratory Anti-Jet-Lag Diet*

COUNTDOWN

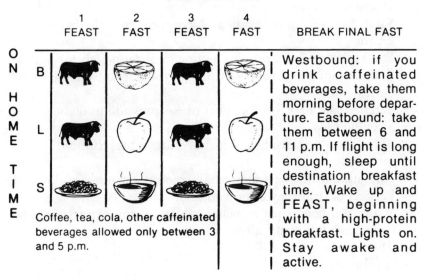

		1 FEAST	2 FAST	3 FEAST	4 FAST	BREAK FINAL FAST

O N   H O M E   T I M E

B

L

S

Coffee, tea, cola, other caffeinated beverages allowed only between 3 and 5 p.m.

Westbound: if you drink caffeinated beverages, take them morning before departure. Eastbound: take them between 6 and 11 p.m. If flight is long enough, sleep until destination breakfast time. Wake up and FEAST, beginning with a high-protein breakfast. Lights on. Stay awake and active.

ARGONNE NATIONAL LABORATORY

ANTI-JET-LAG DIET

The Argonne Anti-Jet-Lag Diet is helping travelers quickly adjust their bodies' internal clocks to new time zones. It is also being used to speed the adjustment of shiftworkers, such as power plant operators, to periodically rotating work hours. The diet was developed by Dr. Charles F. Ehret of Argonne's Division of Biological and Medical Research as an application of his fundamental studies of the daily biological rhythms of animals. Argonne National Laboratory is one of the U. S. Department of Energy's major centers of research in energy and the fundamental sciences. Argonne National Laboratory, 9700 South Cass Avenue, Argonne, Illinois 60439

- Dacriose or other eyewash
- Salve for bug bites, such as Neosporin or a hydrocortisone cream
- Bug repellent and mosquito netting (mosquito coils for burning that contain pyrethrum are usually available outside the United States)
- Sudafed and/or Afrin for relief of ear pressure in flight
- Sleeping pills
- pHisoderm or pHisohex (which requires a prescription) for skin infections
- Any other medicine you normally require on a day-to-day basis
- Packets of oral rehydration solution
- Water purifiers, such as water tablets (iodine-tetraglycine, hydroperiodide), water filters
- Thermometer
- Antibiotics

1.76 Do not take antibiotics without the advice of a doctor. However, if you are traveling to remote areas or to places where it may be difficult to get prescriptions filled, you may ask your doctor to prescribe an antibiotic such as tetracycline, erythromycin, or cephalexin (brand name Keflex) to have with you in case you contract a severe infection. For people who react adversely to antibiotics, tetracycline produces the least reaction, but it comes in capsule form and may melt in hot places. Erythromycin, which may produce a stronger reaction, also comes in capsule form, but it covers a wider range of bacteria. Cephalexin (Keflex), which may produce a reaction, comes in tablet form (good for stability in hot climates) and covers a wide range of bacteria, but it is very expensive.

Other Medical Precautions

1.77 Anticipate your needs for inoculations. Tetanus and cholera shots sometimes produce a strong reaction, and it is unpleasant to travel while you are still feeling the aftereffects. This is an especially important consideration if you are traveling with children. Also, for cholera and typhoid immunization, you will require more than one inoculation; these inoculations must be at least a week apart and *should* be as much as a month apart (see also 1.79).

1.78 You must start taking malaria prophylaxis pills two weeks before departure for them to be effective. Be sure to note the day you must take your next malaria pill on your travel calendar. Also, note on your calendar that you must continue taking malaria pills for six weeks after your departure from a risk area.

Note: In some areas of Africa (especially Kenya and Tanzania), chloroquine has been found ineffective as a prophylaxis for malaria. *Health Information for International Travel,* a publication of the U.S. Department of Health and Human Services (see 1.43) recommends that, in such areas, pyrimethamine and sulfadoxine (brand name Fansidar, which requires a prescription) be used in addition to chloroquine. Other malaria/mosquito defenses—such as mosquito netting, mosquito spray, incense, insect repellent, tape for screen holes—should also be considered, depending on the extremity of need (see also 1.96).

1.79 Under international health regulations, some countries may require immunizations for yellow fever and cholera. This should be checked when you ask about visa requirements (see 1.9).

Note: Doctors who specialize in international health issues have questioned the effectiveness of the cholera vaccine, and several international clinics in the United States will administer it only when it is a requirement of entry or transit.

1.80 Your personal doctor can give you inoculations for tetanus, cholera, and typhoid as well as gamma globulin to help prevent hepatitis. Your doctor can also prescribe prophylaxis pills for malaria. Yellow fever shots are given only at certain medical facilities; your doctor cannot administer them at the office. In the Washington, D.C. area, they are given by the Georgetown University Medical School International Health Service—call (202)625-7379 for an appointment—and by the Johns Hopkins University International Health Clinic—call (301)955-8931 during regular business hours. Elsewhere, you may call your state health department to find out immunizations and clinics that administer yellow fever shots (see also 1.42).

1.81 Record your blood type and Rh factor on a sheet of paper, and tape it into your passport and record it in your notebook. Also carry your vaccination certificate in case you are ill and have to show it to a doctor. Keep a copy of this information in your office or home emergency contingency file (see 1.129 and 1.130).

1.82 Make sure that your health insurance is paid up before you travel and that coverage for illness outside the United States is available (see 1.49–1.55, Health Insurance and Emergency Referral Plans).

1.83 For more extensive health information, a good source is *The Traveler's Health Guide,* by Patrick Doyle, M.D., and James Banta, M.D.—available for about $10 from Acropolis Books, Washington, D.C.; call (301)387-6805.

1.84 If your children are traveling separately from you or are staying at home during your trip, whoever is in charge of them should be provided with a power of attorney authorizing them to permit required emergency operations or treatment if no guardian or other parent is present. Such a document should be kept in your home folder during your trip (see 1.130).

1.85 Be sure that you know how to ask for a doctor (and for the police) in the language of the country you are visiting.

Reservations, Travel Information, and Personal Security

Travel Agents

1.86 Select a travel agent who has overseas experience and regularly handles business clients traveling to your destination. The following questions are useful tests of a good agent:

- Does the agent speak any foreign languages, thereby showing familiarity with conditions and customs encountered outside the United States?
- Does the agent serve business clients and tourists or group tours with diverse overseas travel needs?
- Does the agent have computer links to many airlines (such as the American Airlines Saber system, the United Airlines Apollo system, or the Eastern Airlines Data II system) so that reservations can be made or changed immediately from the agent's office?
- Does the agent have a special line for business clients and 24-hour service?
- Is the agent a member of the American Society of Travel Agents (ASTA), which assures the traveler that the agent has been in business for a period of years and has an established sales volume?

Such an agent should be able to give you the best information on airlines, fares, and lodging. (Some agents now give money-back guarantees on obtaining the lowest fare for their customers.) The agent should also be your first blush guide to personal security needs in any country on your itinerary.

Note: An agent with computer links can deal with reservations efficiently even if you are calling from abroad at an hour when local ticket offices may be closed. This capability allows you to take advantage of the time difference to get a reservation on a crowded or overbooked flight or to cancel or confirm a reservation.

Alternative Sources of Travel, Lodging, and Security Information

1.87 For up-to-the-minute information about the most convenient travel arrangements and accommodations, you may wish to contact people in your country of destination or people who have been there recently. The advantage of talking to such people is not only that you can obtain the most recent information but also that you can ask about conditions—including political conditions—that might affect your personal security. Usually, you are only a few phone calls away from such information. The best sources are:

- Your customer/client/host in your country of destination
- The overseas representative of a U.S. bank that does business in your country of destination or the loan officer in the U.S. bank who covers that country
- The overseas representative of a U.S. company or the officer who handles company business in your country of destination (Listings of U.S. companies in foreign countries are available in *The International Directory of Corporate Affiliations,* published by National Register Publishing Company, available at any central library or, for about $270, from the publisher, 866 Third Avenue, 29th Floor, New York, NY 10022.)
- The office of the U.S. Chamber of Commerce in your country of destination, which can also tell you which American banks and companies do business in the country
- The overseas or local representatives who cover your country of destination for the World Bank—listed (without phone numbers) in the *World Bank Annual Report,* available free from the World Bank, 1818 H Street, N.W., Washington, DC 20433, (202)477-1234

Note: The procedure at the World Bank, for example, would be to call the central telephone number and ask for an officer covering loans to your country of destination. You would then explain to the person answering the phone, usually a secretary, that you are going to city "X" in country "Y" and would like to talk to someone who has been there recently. Specifically, you want to know about any security problems. You will then, most likely, be transferred to the person who can answer your question. If the conversation is pleasant, you can usually proceed to other items on your list of questions and gain more helpful tips (see 1.89).

1.88 As of this writing, changes are under way in the U.S. Department of State that are designed to centralize and speed up the flow of information about terrorist and security threats to American companies and individuals. For example, the Private Sector Liaison

Staff in the Coordination Center of the Diplomatic Security Office plans to establish a computerized electronic bulletin board that will provide up-to-the-minute, unclassified security threat information, including travelers' advisories, through prearranged corporate computer connections. These changes will probably entail organizational realignment and office relocations, so some of the addresses, telephone numbers, and services offered by various offices may change. It is also likely that various divisions will furnish different sorts of security information and will be unaware of other State Department information services. A direct overseas phone call to the embassy or consular officer who handles security matters in your country of destination may be the most informative source, especially in smaller U.S. overseas missions. In larger missions, it may be difficult to find the correct office and to provide satisfactory identification.

Current State Department information sources include the following:

- The Consular Section/Commercial Section/Regional Security Officer (RSO) of the U.S. Embassy in your country of destination is a good source. For names of embassy officers, addresses, and numbers of embassies, see "Key Officers of Foreign Posts/ Guide for U.S. Business Representatives," Department of State Publication 7877, updated three times a year and available from the Superintendent of Documents, U.S. Government Printing Office, Washington, DC 20402. Or you may request information from the country desk officer at the Department of State, through the central telephone number: (202)647-4000. (Expect delays and follow-up calls.)
- The Threat Analysis Division (TAD—part of the Diplomatic Security Office, Policy and Counter Terrorism Office, Office of Policy Coordination)—responds to requests for security information from corporate security representatives; call (202)647-0279.
- The Private Sector Liaison Staff, which reports to the Coordination Center of the Diplomatic Security Office, is designed to provide unclassified daily updated terrorist-related security information to properly identified American corporations with

overseas branches, assets, or operations. An electronic bulletin board available through prearranged computer links is being planned. At present, the number for discussing the availability of such information is (202)647-2412.

- The Office of Training, Diplomatic Security Center, Antiterrorism Program, Publications provides properly identified American corporations or individuals with security information publications, such as *Terrorism: Avoidance and Survival,* available from the Foreign Service Institute, (202)235-9461. (For other security references, see 1.134.)
- Travelers to the Middle East and other places that are considered trouble spots should contact The Citizens Emergency Center (part of the department's Office of Consular Affairs), Room 4811, U.S. Department of State, Washington, DC 20520, (202)647-5225, for updated travel information and advisories.
- The International Airline Passengers Association (IAPA) has introduced a program in 1987 that provides a security guideline report about terrorist incidents worldwide, from the Control Risks Group, a security consulting firm. Subscription to the IAPA Control Risks Programme involves paying an insurance fee of $200 to $300 per year, in addition to the regular IAPA membership fee of about $90 per year. Information about the program is available by calling the IAPA office in Dallas, Texas at 214-520-1070 or 1-800-527-5888 (see also note following 1.54).

Basic Travel Questions to Ask as You Plan Your Trip

1.89   Is there some overriding development in the country that is reason not to go there at all? Obviously, no business traveler or tourist would intentionally go to a place that is anticipating or undergoing major political upheaval. However, anticipating such political upheaval is not always easy. Many American companies with worldwide interests maintain divisions that analyze the political threat. Also, political risk services—such as Frost and Sullivan, 106 Fulton Street, New York, NY 10038, (212)233-1080—publish country-by-country forecasts for subscribers of the probability of political turmoil. If your company has such resources, they should be used as part of your overall security review. The contacts recommended in 1.87, starting with your overseas client, should also be able to alert you to threats of major political trouble. More important, those contacts can probably give you some indication of whether your company, your type of business, and/or foreign business in general is likely to be the target of terrorist attention.

1.90 What is the security situation at the airport? Have there been any plane hijackings there?

1.91 For the business I have to do, what is the most convenient and most reasonably priced (or most luxurious) place to stay? Which is the business hotel; which is the "local color" hotel? Are there hucksters or prostitutes at the hotel? Is it safe to walk in that area of the city?

1.92 What is the best route and the best carrier to use to get there? Is the national airline safe? Is there a different airport nearer the center city? Are there intermediate transit hubs that should be avoided?

1.93 Is there some particular problem or event in the country at the time of my visit that I should prepare for or avoid? For example, have there been a rash of stickups or threatened terrorist activities aimed at U.S. businesses? Is the government inhospitable to foreign or American business or to any particular business activities? Are there any scheduled national holidays, religious holidays, strikes, visits by the Pope, large Shriners' conventions, World Cup soccer matches, and so forth?

1.94 Are there any details that travelers should be particularly wary of in the country? For example, do airport cabs charge different, higher rates (but no tips)? Are passports needed for internal travel? Is a famous museum open only on certain days? Have the currency denominations changed so that 1,000 pesos is now 100 pesos—and will cabbies try to take advantage of the unknowing? Are the local authorities cracking down on illegal currency exchanges, religious customs, laws related to dress or to bringing in *Playboy* or liquor?

1.95 What clothes are appropriate for various activities or for leisure time? Are any clothes that Americans commonly use inappropriate (for example, bush jackets in Rio de Janeiro)? Special care should be taken to determine acceptable dress codes for women traveling to Arab states. Also, many countries require women to wear long skirts and prohibit shorts—Malawi, for example.

1.96 Are there any particular health problems or medical needs to anticipate? Is water potable in cities and rural areas? Is some bug going around? Is there a shortage of common medical supplies, such as sterile syringes? Is the altitude a problem? For travel to Africa and other areas where medical resources are scarce and overextended, you will want to ask about blood-screening procedures and about malaria that is not preventable by chloroquine prophylaxis.

1.97 The following are other country-specific considerations you should ask about:

- What are the tipping customs? Often, a 10 percent service fee is already included in European and Latin American bills, although some additional gratuity is usually expected.
- Are any items prohibited for import or likely to be confiscated by customs?
- What is the local electrical current for appliances? Is an adapter required for radios, hairdryers, and the like?
- What is the cab situation from the airport to the hotel? (For example, cabs travel in caravans at night to thwart roadside bandits in Lagos, Nigeria, and Georgetown, Guyana.)
- Are small, inexpensive items from the United States that are not available on the local market suitable for small gifts?
- For remote or unusual destinations, are maps readily available, or should they be purchased in advance in the United States?
- Are activities available for spouses traveling with business executives whose business dealings will occupy most of the visit? (Bear in mind that if the spouse is a wife, the wives of the

foreign business hosts may volunteer to entertain her. Their idea of fun may be too "home-oriented" for the taste of American women, however, so you might ask about some alternatives.)
- Is there some feature, museum, or show in the country that should not be missed?

Basic Security Considerations in Choosing a Hotel

You should consider your hotel reservation exclusively from the point of view of your personal security. This is especially true after the U.S. air raid on Tripoli, Libya, in April 1986. An experienced travel agent can be very helpful in responding to the security considerations outlined above. Your object is to find lodging where terrorists are unlikely to plant a bomb and where it would be difficult for you to be spotted by a terrorist surveillant.

1.98 If you want to stay at a large, first-class hotel where American and other foreign senior executives are known to congregate, consider that such a hotel might be a terrorist target—although protective security is likely to be tighter there, and the limited time you would usually spend at the hotel would reduce your risk.

1.99 Avoid staying in a hotel next to a likely terrorist target, such as the U.S. Embassy, the Israeli Embassy (or their respective ambassadors' residences), the headquarters of a U.S. multinational company or bank, or a government building likely to attract separatist terrorist fire.

1.100 Conversely, do select a hotel near a central police station, near the Vatican Embassy or the Saudi Arabian Embassy, or, if there is no separatist threat, near the president's office or residence.
   Note: This suggestion may have risks. Only those with a thorough knowledge of the area should attempt to predict which targets terrorists would consider untouchable.

1.101 If you are in a business that might single you out for individual terrorist attention, you might want to find a large hotel with much activity and several exits, so that a terrorist surveillant would find it difficult to observe your comings and goings. Alternatively, you might want to find a small, little-known hotel (where the guest list would not be an objective of terrorist intelligence) on a side street with little activity, so that any surveillant would be conspicuous, and authorities could be alerted.

Note: At any hotel, it is safer to register in your own name, without identifying any corporate or institutional affiliation (see 1.107).

1.102 The availability of taxis—in line in front of your hotel or readily available by telephone request—is a security consideration if travel on foot is inadvisable (see also 4.23 and 4.24, Choosing a Taxi).

1.103 Direct access to the subway line from the hotel lobby, or ready access without public exposure, may be an important security factor (see also 4.21, Local Transportation).

1.104 If you are invited to stay in an apartment or a house during your foreign visit, you should review the same security considerations. An apartment is likely to have the additional security of a concierge, and a house will often have an outside protective wall (and your host may provide transport to your business by car).

Note: Your hotel or apartment is not the likely starting point for any terrorist surveillance. Such spotting and surveillance might well start when you emerge from the country club, having played tennis with the local head of Black and Decker, or when you come out of the American Club after lunch with your prominent business client or with a U.S. Embassy official. Your selection of a hotel or apartment should be calculated to make it as difficult as possible for a potential terrorist assailant to track your pattern of behavior and to know where to find you (see 5.54, Signs of Surveillance).

1.105 If your visit will place you in regular contact with someone who is a likely target of terrorist attention, remember that your safety will depend on your host's security precautions when you are with him or her. Before accepting an invitation, you should consider the risks that might be involved and how they might be reduced. Your personal security is only as good as your host's (see 5.42).

1.106 In countries where fire safety is not given high priority, you may want to find out whether your hotel has a sprinkler system— or ask your travel agent to check. At present, the use of smoke detectors in hotels outside the United States, especially in less developed countries, is not common.

1.107 Make your hotel reservations in your own name to help keep you inconspicuous and to avoid your association with any institution of possible interest to terrorists. For purposes of security and so that future correspondence will arrive at your office, register in your own name, but use your office address.

1.108 As the date of your departure approaches, you should call to confirm your hotel reservations. Get the name of the person you talk to (or ask whoever is making the call on your behalf in a foreign tongue to get the name).

1.109 In reviewing the security criteria for your hotel, you should not fail to ask someone familiar with local political conditions about your hotel. From all physical standpoints, the choice may be a safe one, but a savvy local resident will know that the hotel is the place where some controversial political leader has his lunch every day; that the hotel is the hangout for the American press corps; or that the hotel is owned by a conservative union pension fund or a prominent Israeli. Part of your overall security review should include a question about matters that only a local person might know.

Air Travel Pointers

1.110 As a security measure, it is wiser to book direct flights, avoiding intermediate stops, so that there are fewer chances for terrorist access to the plane.

1.111   Book passage on airlines that are not likely to be objects of terrorist attention (for example, avoid TWA, Pan Am, and El Al, which have been targets for recent terrorist attacks) and on flights that avoid airports known for lax security.

Note: The choice of airlines and flights is not simple, and there are trade-offs to be considered. For example, El Al is considered to maintain the most rigid security standards worldwide and has successfully foiled several serious threats recently; and Pan Am has instituted an extensive security procedure for its international flights, probably including computer profiles of passengers who might be terrorists—like procedures on the Concorde. Furthermore, the weakest link in the security chain is likely to be the airport and the airport's security of access to international flights—not the airline. Thus, the security record of the airports where a flight stops is more important than the choice of airline or flag of carrier. There are expensive corporate security services that provide information about airports, but the quickest way to check is to call the U.S. Department of State, Citizens Emergency Center, (202)647-5225, where a country desk officer can give you a travelers' advisory on any country you ask about. If an airport in that country has been a problem, it will be in the advisory (see also 1.87 and 1.88). The problem, of course, is knowing where the lightning will strike next, not where it has already struck.

1.112   Paying full fare gives you the flexibility to change your flights without paying a penalty and without being held to a particular airline or time.

1.113   Avoid charters, which could put you on a flight with a group that might be a terrorist target (for example, the Brandeis University alumni charter on Pan Am from New York to Athens to see Greek ruins). Also avoid charter airlines that are likely to be targets of terrorist attention.

1.114   Unless there is some reason not to do so, always make a reservation for a return flight. This is especially important if you are traveling to a remote destination or are planning side trips to small towns that have few flights (or where weather conditions commonly restrict air travel). This precaution will keep you from being trapped in some airport awaiting an opening and will ensure that you will be first in line for the next available flight.

1.115 If possible, take the extra time on your arrival at the airport to confirm your return flight—especially in remote or small cities. This will avoid your having to find the ticket office—invariably on the other side of town from your hotel and open only at inconvenient times. Often, such services cannot be handled by phone and cannot be done reliably by hotel travel agents unless the airline has an office in the hotel. At luxury hotels, the concierge can take care of such tasks easily (see also 4.6).

1.116 Even if you do not normally travel first class, travel first class on small connecting flights or on side trips, so that if your flight is delayed or canceled, the airline will put you up in a decent hotel, not a flea bag.
   Note: This advice conflicts with recommended seating for safety (see 3.8–3.10). You will have to choose between comfort and safety.

Rail Travel Pointers

1.117 In many countries, the most efficient and comfortable means of travel is by rail. Also, trains are much less likely to be hijacked. Trains deliver you to center city and, in many countries, are unfailingly prompt. You should consider the rail alternative in planning your trip—it is often the most picturesque means of travel.

1.118 If possible, buy tickets ahead of time through a travel agent—not just before boarding at the station—to avoid long lines, language misunderstandings, and the risks of a jostling crowd for a conspicuous foreigner.

1.119 In Europe, where there are relatively short distances between major cities and an excellent rail system, trains are the most practical and least expensive means of travel for a lone traveler. For a family or group of four or five, however, sharing an auto rental may cut travel costs and increase scheduling flexibility.

1.120 Eurailpass and similar rail passes in other parts of the world provide cost-competitive—and luxurious—travel for long-distance travelers who plan to log many miles per day. However, individual tickets from place to place or on a set course of travel over an extended period are considerably cheaper than Eurailpass. For information on Eurailpass, write to Eurailpass, Box 325, Old Greenwich, CT 06870-0325 or call CIT Tours, (212)397-2667; French National Railroads, (212)582-2110; or Germanrail, (212)308-3100.

Names and Numbers to Know in Emergencies

1.121 Before the last-minute rush prior to travel, you may wish to prepare a list of contacts you might need in an emergency:

- The name of the U.S. ambassador or consul in the country and city of destination and the 24-hour telephone number of the U.S. mission—available by calling the State Department, (202)647-4000, and asking for the country desk of your destination
- The addresses and phone numbers for American Express and other issuers of traveler's checks at off-hours, in case your traveler's checks are lost or stolen. (See 1.33 for a list of emergency numbers to call when traveler's checks are lost.)

1.122 It would be wise to tape a sheet of paper containing this information (and your blood type and Rh factor) on the back page of your passport. Make sure that any family members traveling with you also have this information taped in the back of their passport. Also keep a copy of the information in the back of any documentation you use when you are not carrying your passport.

*Other Travel Cautions: Illegal Drugs and Off-Limits
Photographs*

1.123 Don't carry illegal drugs. Your constitutional rights don't work outside the United States, and most countries have harsh laws to punish those caught with illegal drugs. Arrest and detention overseas can be extremely dangerous, and the U.S. Embassy will be limited in its ability to help (see 5.69).

Note: The State Department reported that more than 900 Americans abroad were arrested in 1985 for violations of local narcotics laws, including possession of marijuana and cocaine. The average age of the Americans arrested was 33 for men and 30 for women. Seventy percent of the arrests were in Jamaica, Mexico, Bahamas, the Dominican Republic, and West Germany.

1.124 Photographers must know what is off-limits for photographs in each country. For example, it is illegal to photograph bridges, government buildings, and radio or TV stations in Israel, Egypt, Lebanon, Spain, and other Mediterranean countries. Airports and seaports, police, soldiers, and civil disturbances are often off-limits for photographers in many African and Latin American countries. In communist countries, the list of photographic restrictions is much longer, and the penalties are more severe. It also may be imprudent to take pictures of the architectural details of a downtown bank or of a foreign embassy building in a country where there has been terrorist activity. Think about the security implications of your photos before you find yourself having to explain to a security guard or a policeman. If in doubt, call the Consulate Office at the U.S. Embassy or Consulate (see also 5.66 and 5.69).

*Anticipating a Terrorist Incident: Preparing Your Family
and Office to Act in an Emergency*

1.125   Before your departure, you should plan with your office
and with your family what is to be done if you are kidnapped or
involved in a hijacking. Such a plan should consider legal, financial,
personnel, public relations, and insurance aspects of the crisis. The
plan should establish the company officer or team that will manage
the crisis and should outline whether an outside firm will be
approached without regard to the State Department, whether a
ransom should be paid, and whether present insurance coverage is
adequate or more should be considered. (The IRS has ruled that
ransom payments for key employees qualify as corporate theft–loss
deductions; see Letter Ruling 7946010.) Any such contingency plan
should be placed in a secure file in your home and office before your
departure.

1.126   You should also consider psychological preparation for
dealing with being a terrorist captive, either on an airplane or as a
kidnap victim. Books on this subject are discussed in 1.134. The
best is *One American Must Die: A Hostage's Personal Account of
the Hijacking of Flight 847,* by Kurt Carlson.

1.127   This manual is aimed at reducing the traveler's risk and
averting disaster. It does not cover negotiations with kidnappers
nor corporate policy in managing such crises. Some publications
that deal with this subject are discussed in 1.134. An insurance plan
that covers such risks is discussed in the note following 1.54 under
Health Insurance and Emergency Referral Plans.

Itinerary and Emergency Communications Plans

1.128   Maintain a file at your office and at home that contains
items needed during an emergency, a terrorist hijacking, or a
kidnapping. Key items in this file are an itinerary and an emergency
communications plan. The itinerary would be the first alert that the
traveler is on a flight that has been hijacked; the emergency
communications plan would be essential later, if the traveler is held
captive. Examples of codes for emergency communications are
given in 1.131.

What to Include in Your Office Folder

1.129   The following items should be kept in your office file while you are traveling:

- Your itinerary, including flight numbers and hours of departure
- A photocopy of your airline ticket (especially, note the ticket number in case it is lost and you seek a replacement or reimbursement)
- A photocopy of your passport (including pages with visas and entry/exit stamps, in case these might attract unfavorable terrorist attention)
- A record of your blood type and Rh factor
- A list of any special health conditions or medicinal restrictions (including the name and phone number of your family doctor and health plan emergency details)
- Your eyeglass prescription
- A photocopy of your vaccination certificate
- A photocopy or list of traveler's check numbers
- An emergency communications plan (see 1.131)
- An overall office plan if you are hijacked or held hostage (including an indication of who will form the "crisis management team" during the crisis, as discussed in 1.125)

The following additional items might also be included:

- Bank deposit slips for your account for company use in your absence
- A brief write-up of the activities you have planned for the trip (so that your explanations to terrorists will be exactly the same as what the office can give to negotiators, to the U.S. Department of State, or to the press)
- A note regarding what information, if any, is to be given to the press (if this is different from the preceding item)
- An AIDS emergency evacuation plan and insurance policy (see 1.49–1.55)

As part of your itinerary, you may wish to preschedule calls to the office or to your home so that a missed call can signal trouble.

What to Include in Your Home Folder

1.130   The following items should be kept in a file at home while you are traveling:

- A valid will, especially including a specified permanent guardian for minor children if their parents die. Most law firms are prepared for last-minute requests for a will and have standard forms to satisfy the legal requirements of your state.
- A record of financial affairs that require administration, including a list of bankers, brokers, and/or lawyers who handle such affairs and provisions for paying utility and phone bills
- A power of attorney over your financial affairs to your spouse or a designated person (also including authorization powers for children's medical emergencies)
- Checks and deposit slips for your joint account (a power of attorney is not valid when you are dead, whereas a joint account may still be used by your spouse or by any designated signer to the joint account)
- Your key to a joint safe deposit box
- A photocopy of your credit cards
- A credit card for your spouse in his or her own name, if not already established
- Copies of your life insurance and health insurance policies
- Your itinerary (same as the office folder, 1.129)
- Instructions about what to do in case of a hijacking or kidnapping: who to contact, what to say to the press—or how to avoid saying anything to the press ("company policy against giving interviews," "I'm too distressed to speak to anyone," and so forth)
- An emergency communications plan (see 1.131).

Developing Code Words for Emergency Communications

1.131 Make a list of key words or a code, and file it at your office and at home in case you are kidnapped and your terrorist captors permit you to speak to outsiders by phone or to write. The list should be short and simple, since you will have to memorize it if it is to deceive your captors.

To help you remember the code list, the first letters of the words on the list should form a simple acronym. For example:

Code Word	True Meaning	Phrase as Spoken or Written
Sad	I am being beaten or tortured.	"*sad* to miss you"
Health(y)	I am injured or sick.	"I'm in good *health*," "I am *healthy*"
Alarmed	I am in a city area with street noises.	"Don't be *alarmed*."
Lonely	I am in a rural area with no street noises.	"I am *lonely* for you."
O.K.	I am O.K., treated well.	"I am *O.K.*"
Many thanks	I am among many armed captors.	"*Many thanks* for your love and support."

Note that the first letters of *sad, health, alarmed, lonely, O.K.,* and *many (thanks)* spell out *SHALOM* and that the code words have some association with (or opposition to) their meaning. Such words will not attract the attention of captors but may assist in locating you or in giving details useful in negotiating your release.

If you are a likely target for terrorist attention, memorizing such a code should have high priority on your list of security measures. Simpler and briefer codes can be devised; for example, leaving out your middle initial in signing a letter or giving your middle initial on the phone in signing on may be given a meaning. Your office should know the code you would use, and your family should also be prepared before you depart.

There is nothing definitive in the sample code words given here. It would be best to make up a simple code that will be easy for you to recall so that you can convey whatever message you find vital, such as a need for a medicine.

Publicity and Security

1.132   Some foreign newspapers and trade journals written for the business community publish items about the visits of foreign business people to the country. Such announcements, often arranged by the local office of a U.S. company, are intended to prepare customers for the visit. If you are a possible terrorist target, you should avoid such publicity at all costs. Similarly, avoid press photos of you and your family.

1.133   If such publicity is an important part of your overseas sales strategy, any announcement should give only an office telephone number to call for an appointment to talk to you. For unknown clients, you or your office should determine where and when any meeting is to take place. Check unknown prospective clients by verifying their status with the companies they claim to represent.

Any publicity about you should give no details about your arrival or departure dates, your hotel or lodging, or your itinerary before you arrive or after you leave. Such information should be held confidentially by you and your company staff.

Recommended Reading

1.134   The following is an annotated list of references that provide useful security information for international travelers:

1. "Hostage Taking: Preparation, Avoidance, and Survival," Department of State Publication 9400, Department of Foreign Service Series 390, Office of Security (October 1984). This manual, written for State Department personnel who are to be posted overseas with their families for an extended period, is excellent for Americans who plan to live abroad in a country where there is a terrorist threat.
2. "Hostage Negotiation in Incidents Involving International Terrorism," by Thomas C. McGrath, Office of Security, Department of State (February 1984); and "Hostage Negotiation: A Matter of Life and Death," Office of Security, Department of State (October 1983).
3. "Terrorism: Avoidance and Survival," Foreign Service Institute, Department of State. This manual is available to security officers of private U.S. companies, with proper identification, by contacting the Department of State Office of

Training, (202)235-9461. This fourteen-page manual is very general and is clearly aimed at American officials who plan to reside in foreign countries for extended periods.
4. "Countering Terrorism," Department of State Publication 8884, originally released in 1977 with recent updates from the Office of Security, Bureau of Administration. This short pamphlet is very general and aimed to serve Americans living abroad.

Note: References 1 through 4 provide a good summary of current information about terrorist hostage taking and kidnapping and include extensive bibliographies of additional information about post-terrorist incident survival. Although these publications are not classified, they are not issued as standard U.S. Government Printing Office items, and they may be limited in circulation.

5. "A Safe Trip Abroad," U.S. Department of State, Bureau of Consular Affairs Publication 9493 (July 1986), available from the Superintendent of Documents, Congressional Sales Office, Washington, DC 20402, and from any U.S. Passport Office, free of charge. This publication gives very general advice, most of which is provided in this guide.
6. *One American Must Die: A Hostage's Personal Account of the Hijacking of Flight 847,* by Kurt Carlson (1986), available from Congdon and Weed, 298 Fifth Avenue, New York, NY, 10001, for about $15.
7. "Hostage Survival," in *Conflict,* Vol. 1, Nos. 1 and 2, by Brooks McClure (1978), available from Crane, Russak and Company, 3 E. 44th Street, New York, NY 10017.
8. *The American Hostage: To Be Or Not To Be* (1986), available from Varicon International, 3 Skyline Place, 5201 Leesburg Pike, Suite 200, Falls Church, VA 22041-3203, for about $10. This book gives advice on hostage conduct during captivity and provides some good general hints.
9. *Everything You Need To Know Before You're Hijacked,* by Dan McKinnon (1986), available from House of Hits Publications, P.O. Box D14, San Diego, CA 92115, for about $8. This book contains much valuable new information about airport security, travel security tips, and how to behave if you are kidnapped. It lacks an index.
10. *Travel Safety—Don't Be A Target* (1987), Uniquest Publications, 2021 St. Estephe Court, Coeur d'Alene, ID 83814. This pocket-sized guide provides an excellent checklist for the safety-conscious traveler. The index is so comprehensive, however, that you have to read everything under a heading to find an individual item of interest.
11. *Executive Safety and International Terrorism: A Guide for Travelers,* by Anthony J. Scotti (1986), available from Prentice-Hall, Inc., Englewood Cliffs, NJ 07632, for about $20. This book—the work of a security specialist—focuses on the terrorist threat to American business and to American officials living and

traveling abroad. The business executive who wants to become a security expert—about armored vehicles and guard dogs—should study this book.

12. "A Minimanual on Surviving Business Trips!" by Keith Wilkins, in the October 1986 issue of *The Internal Auditor: Journal of the Institute of Internal Auditors,* 249 Maitland Avenue, Altamonte Springs, FL 32701. This article is an excellent brief on how the business traveler should deal with the terrorist threat. Some minor points should be adopted with extreme caution; for example, "Use an alias or a modification of your name when making your [hotel] reservations" would make it difficult for an embassy to locate you in an emergency, and there is bound to be confusion when you check into the hotel using documents with a different name from the reservation. The article's overall analysis, however, makes it worth reading.

2
What to Take on Your Trip

A Shopping List of Essentials

2.1 All experienced travelers recommend traveling light and carrying only what you really need or what is unlikely to be available abroad. You should plan to take no more luggage than you can carry comfortably by yourself, as many places may not have porters—or may have unreliable volunteer porters—and conditions may not be suitable for portable, wheeled bag carriers.

2.2 The following are lists of items many experienced travelers have found useful to have in their carry-on travel bags or to carry in their pockets. Also included are some very small and light items that would help a traveler on land after an airplane has been downed. These lists have been designed to avoid items that might attract terrorist attention or suspicion. Clearly, some items are inappropriate for certain destinations; travelers should evaluate their needs before deciding which items to carry. Also note that couples or families traveling together can distribute supplies among their bags so that no one person has to carry everything and duplication can be avoided.

There is a temptation in preparing for a trip to buy a lot of new gizmos and luggage. Unless you really need and plan to use an item, avoid this temptation. Using familiar items, such as your daily notebook, pocket calculator, penknife, and hand luggage will maintain your routine and avoid surprises. Also, test new items, such as a new hair dryer, traveling iron, or travel alarm clock to see that they work and that you understand their operation.

Travel Guides

2.3 The following small items are necessities for the international traveler:

- A pocket dictionary or foreign phrase book (Be sure to look up the words for "Help!" "fire" "doctor," and "police.")
- A small map and tourist guide (Weather maps snipped from local daily newspapers often show major cities, provinces, and regions, so larger maps are unnecessary unless you require a detailed city street map—indispensable, for example, for Paris or São Paulo.)
- A one-page metric conversion table for weights, measures, and temperatures (often found in lead pages of travel diaries; also metric equivalents at the end of this book)

Schedules, Addresses, and Notebooks

2.4 Take a pocket-sized daily schedule book as well as a pocket-sized notebook and address book. Spiral-bound schedule books are handier than bound or stapled books, as you can hold them open with one hand while talking on the phone. These books should be different from the ones you use in the United States in case they are lost. Also, if you are carrying important addresses, leave a photocopy of the address book at home or have a separate copy with you in case of theft or loss.

2.5 A pad of 3M Post-it note pads is useful for attaching corrections or notations to the pages of your daily schedule. Although record-keeping styles differ, it is often useful to have space on your daily schedule pages to note expense items and other things you want to remember.

2.6 Review all notebook entries and addresses as if you will have to justify them to a terrorist. For example, if you know the U.S. ambassador or other prominent figure personally, do not include the first names of his or her spouse and children in your address book so that a terrorist would not perceive your friendship. Also be sure that the entries do not look like a secret code, which might require some uncomfortable explanations.

Appliances/Electrical Items

2.7 You will need an electricity adapter for wall outlets so that your electrical appliances will work on foreign voltage. A compact adapter is available from the Boston Proper catalogue (item 1256), 1-800-243-4300, for about $27.

European outlet plugs (with two round tines), with converters for U.S. appliance plugs, are also available.

Note: An adapter will solve voltage problems but may not handle electric motor cycle differences. Thus, some sensitive appliances that will have heavy use should be purchased abroad.

2.8 The following electrical items are very useful while traveling:

- Batteries for camera, wristwatch, small flashlight, calculator
- A penlight flashlight (with pocket clip)—available from the Brookstone Company catalogue, (603)924-9541, for about $7—or the watch fob, ten-year, tiny flashlight—available from the Paragon Catalogue, (401)596-0134, for about $15
- A small calculator
- A small hair dryer
- A travel iron—the Rowanta Folding Travel Iron, available from the Boston Proper catalogue (item 6513), 1-800-243-4300, for about $50; or the Mini Travel Iron, available from the Travel Store catalogue, 1-800-854-6677, for about $20
- A travel alarm clock—the compact Braun travel clock, about 3″ x 3″ x 1″, available from the Boston Proper catalogue (item 2145), 1-800-243-4300, for about $40; or the compact International Travel Alarm, about 2½″ x 3″ x ⅜″, available from the L.L. Bean catalogue (item 8658KK), 1-800-221-4221, for about $25

Note: Take batteries out of radios, flashlights, and so on, while traveling so that there is no risk that the appliances will be turned on in your luggage during the trip, exhausting the batteries.

Toiletries and Convenience Items

2.9 The following items will be necessary on your trip:

- A toothbrush, toothpaste, shaving kit (with extra blades), and comb
- Soap and a plastic soap container
- Nonliquid shampoo in a nonleak tube
- Solid stick or cream deodorant (nonliquid so as not to leak)
- A roll of toilet paper in a zip-lock plastic bag (a partially used roll is less bulky, and the inner core can be removed to save space)
- Tissues for covering toilet seats—a package of sixty Sani-Seat covers is available from Brookstone's Homewares catalogue (item J-11955), (603)924-9541, for about $8
- Tampons and/or sanitary napkins
- Chapstick
- Sun lotion
- Woolite—available in small packets in powder form
- Safety pins
- Several zip-lock plastic bags—for any medicines or liquid items that might leak, for your washcloth, for holding materials such as pamphlets or books that must be kept dry, or for keeping dirty items separate in your luggage
- Prepackaged moist towelettes—especially for cleaning newspaper ink from your fingers
- A small shoehorn
- A large handkerchief
- A braided, stretchable line for drying wet garments without pins for hanging—Flexo-line is available from Le Travel Store catalogue, 1-800-854-6677, for about $5
- An inflatable drip-dry hanger for hanging washed shirts to dry in the bathroom—also available from Le Travel Store catalogue, 1-800-854-6677
- A plastic hanger with clips (or two clothespins) to hang out washed undies, socks
- A plastic bag for carrying dirty laundry—a plastic hotel laundry bag will usually do

- A traveler's needle and thread kit, with extra shirt buttons
- Brass or plastic collar stays
- Cuff links
- A fold-up umbrella—a nine-inch-long folding umbrella is available from Hammacher Schlemmer (item 24009R), 1-800-543-3366, for about $30

Note: Frequent travelers often keep a separate toiletries and medicines bag packed and ready to go, so that these items do not have to be reassembled for each trip.

Medical Items

2.10 It will be important to have the following medicines and other medical items with you (see 1.75 and 1.76):

- Aspirin or a substitute, such as Tylenol
- A pain killer prescribed by your doctor, such as Darvocet
- Medicine for diarrhea (see 1.63 and 1.64)
- A laxative
- Cold pills, such as Dristan or Contac
- A collapsible drinking cup
- An antibiotic prescription, such as tetracycline, erythromycin, or cephalexein (see 1.76, Antibiotics)
- Dacriose or other eyewash
- Band-Aids
- Tweezers
- A syringe and needle (3-5 cubic centimeter syringe and 3-5 gauge needle) in a sterile packet—available at most major drug outlets (may require a prescription and should be noted in a doctor's certificate so that customs officials will not think it is narcotics paraphernalia); especially important in areas where there is a risk of AIDS from improperly decontaminated syringes at health facilities (see 1.56–1.58, AIDS)
- A small roll of surgical tape
- Mercurochrome or other antiseptic, such as Bacitracin, for open cuts or blisters
- Sudafed and/or Afrin for ear pressure in flight

- Ointment or salve for bug bites, such as Neosporin or a hydrocortisone cream
- Sleeping pills
- Water purification tablets—available at sporting goods and Army-Navy stores—or tinctured iodine (one drop in a pint of water for three minutes produces potable water)
- Sunglasses or a plastic shade that fits over your eyeglasses
- Mosquito netting (where needed) or bug repellant
- An extra pair of your glasses or reading glasses (or extra contact lenses and contact lens solution)
- Chewing gum
- Chocolate bars (in zip-lock plastic bag)
- Life Savers
- A thermometer (electronic preferred over mercury)

Security Items

2.11   The following items may be useful for thwarting assault and theft:

- A Velcro and nylon wallet (about passport size) that can be attached to your belt loop or shoulder strap to keep valuables under your clothes—the Flip Away is available from Le Travel Store catalogue, 1-800-854-6677, for about $12; a similar wallet is available from the Comfortably Yours catalogue, (201)368-0400, for about $10; and Bean's Security Pocket, about 8″ x 6″, is available from L.L. Bean, 1-800-341-4341, for about $8. **Note:** In hot climates, use a zip-lock plastic liner for hidden wallets so that your money and documents aren't drenched with sweat.
- A money belt with a zipper on the inner lining—available from the Brookstone Company catalogue (item C-03514A), (603) 924-9541, for about $20
- Large safety pins for pinning cash inside pockets or inside a purse (especially useful for women's dress or skirt pockets)
- A small strand of bendable wire, such as coat hanger wire, to fix baggage handles if they break
- A three-foot-long piece of nonstretch clothesline or strong string to replace broken bag handles—several strands thick so that it won't cut into your hand

- A small roll of fiber tape or nonrip tape to repair ripped or broken luggage
- A cheap wristwatch (valuable watches make you a target for street thieves) and washable wrist bands
- An attachable door lock to use inside the hotel room door where a door chain is not provided by the hotel—available from the Brookstone Company catalogue (item C-09708), (603)924-9541, for about $15
- A book safe for storing valuables in your hotel room—easily made by cutting out the inner pages of a thick paperback, or available from the Brookstone Company catalogue (item C-10814), (603)924-9541, for about $20

Note: Le Travel Store catalogue, 1-800-854-6677 (during working hours, Pacific Time), has several alternatives to these recommendations, as well as other travelers' aids.

Some people take the extra precaution to taping a strip or two of metal banding inside the bottom of any tote bag or large purse to be used while shopping overseas. An alternative is to put a coat hanger wire, bent in a zig-zag pattern, on the bottom of the bag. This thwarts street thieves, who may try to cut open the bottom of your bag or purse with a razor while accomplices are jostling you in a crowd.

2.12 The most useful item to have with you in case of emergency is a pocket knife, such as a Swiss Army knife that includes scissors, a corkscrew, a can opener, a bottle opener, and a screw driver as well as blades.

Note: Any pocket knife (except for the compact, blade-and-screwdriver-only version that usually won't set off a metal detector) should be carried inside your hand luggage. Under present airport security, a pocket knife that is pulled from your pocket when you go through a metal detector may be held by airline staff during the flight and returned to you after arrival. It may be advisable to carry a corkscrew, can opener, bottle opener, and scissors separately in case your pocket knife is noted and removed from your luggage. Carry the scissors in your toilet kit, or use the fold-up variety, available from the Hoffritz catalogue, 1-800-962-9699, for about $35. Otherwise, they, too may be taken from your luggage.

Other useful items in case of emergency are:

- A small pocket compass—the Zip-clip compass is available from the Eddie Bauer catalogue, 1-800-426-8020, for about $4
- A tiny, 10-year flashlight with ring clip—available from the Paragon catalogue, (401)596-0134, for about $15—or a penlight flashlight (see 2.8)
- A metal reflecting mirror (Army-Navy store type)
- A small magnifying glass
- Matches in a zip-lock bag
- Medical items listed in 2.10, especially water purification tablets
- A small, wide-based candle

Note: In 3.18, there is reference to an emergency smoke hood—for evacuating a smoke-filled plane. In Europe, there is a fire and smoke escape mask marketed under the brand named Vivat, which is sold through Woodville Polymer Engineering, Ltd., Heathcote Rd., Swadlincote, Burton on Trent, Staffordshire, U.K., DE 11-9DX, Attn: Peter Shrubsall. Call 283-22-11-22. An American model, RESQ I and RESQ II, will be marketed in the United States in 1988. Inquiries should be addressed to Intech, 6611 Waterwood Trail, Fort Worth, TX 76132, 817-731-2915. This item, which is a plastic hood with a passive filter placed in front of the wearer's mouth, is easy to use and carry and fits easily into luggage or a pocket. It is sold in a plastic envelope measuring 5½" x 8" and weighs less than five ounces. This product is a must for frequent air travelers and for those who want additional protection from smoke in hotels or office buildings.

2.13 Review all items you plan to carry to be sure that they are consistent with the business or tourist purpose of your trip and that they do not suggest that you might be associated with the U.S. Embassy or the military or even that you have served in the military. (See also 3.20 regarding carrying your passport in your hand luggage and delaying presentation to terrorists.)

Note: Several security specialists suggest it may be prudent to carry a pocket edition of the King James version of the Bible, including the New Testament, or other Christian religious objects in your hand luggage, especially when your name or destination might lead Arab terrorists to believe you are Jewish.

Items to Carry for Business

2.14 Security specialists suggest that you use soft luggage instead of a briefcase so that hijackers will not perceive you as a business traveler who may be valuable as a hostage. A carry-on bag with a shoulder strap, which is not so obviously a business item, can accommodate a business case inside (see 2.20). The Strong Soft Briefcase, for example, is available from the Eddie Bauer catalogue (item M198B), 1-800-426-8020, for about $50.

2.15 The following business items will be essential:

- Extra office stationery for writing revised commitment letters to clients or new letters
- An extra canvas tote bag (foldable) for carrying bulky catalogues back from your business trip or for carrying bulk items to clients (then folding and packing for the return trip)
- Extra calling cards (for nonbusiness travel, you may wish to carry personal cards with your home address and phone)
- An extra business shirt and tie, or extra blouse, in case your baggage is lost by the airline
- A business-related alternative to the Swiss Army knife, which includes a pocket stapler, a hole punch, a tape measure, a magnifying glass, scissors, and blades—The Factory is available from the Boston Proper catalogue (item 6512), 1-800-243-4300, for about $35; a similar item is available from the Hoffritz catalogue, 1-800-962-9699. Note that multiple-function tools often perform no single function as well as an individual stapler, penknife or magnifying glass.

Other (Optional) Items

2.16 Other useful items to have with you are:

- "Escape literature"—reading material for when you are delayed unexpectedly in an airport for several hours—or a crossword puzzle book and/or miniature playing cards
- A pair of pliers and a screwdriver

- A camera with a flash attachment and film
- An indelible ink pen (for labeling poster tubes or boxes of material acquired on the trip)
- A plastic or tough paper extendable poster tube for architectural drawings or posters
- A suitcase organizer with hanger and plastic containers— available from the Joan Cook catalogue, 1-800-327-3799, for about $15
- Shoe trees
- A pants hanger
- A small shoeshine kit
- A tennis racket or other athletic equipment
- Condoms
- Family photographs for wallet
- A flask or bottle of any favorite liquor that is not available overseas (for example, sour mash whiskey other than Jack Daniels)
- Smelling salts
- A styptic pencil to stop small cuts (as from shaving) from bleeding
- A swimsuit—especially useful if your flight is diverted to some hot climate or you have an unexpected layover in Jamaica
- A Hide-a-Key, a small metal box with magnet attached that is useful for hiding things in your hotel room. (A hollowed out paperbook book may also serve as a quick hiding place for valuables.)
- An electrical converter that will allow you to plug a U.S. appliance into a light bulb socket
- Ear plugs—for noise or for swimming
- Tub stoppers (rubber wafer style)—some foreign hotels do not have stoppers
- Cotton swabs (Q-tips) and cotton balls (if not likely to be available abroad)
- Barrettes, extra earring backs

Necessary Items If You Are Traveling with Children

2.17 The foregoing lists do not take into account those who are traveling with young children. The essential constant when traveling with children is to try to keep a routine so that the upsetting effects of unpredictable change are held to a minimum. This attempt to maintain a routine in the midst of movement, changing schedules, and unusual activities dictates that you carry items that will help keep your aggravation level down and will keep your children comfortable and among some familiar, treasured items. Your list should include the following key items:

- A portable stroller. A sturdy model is the Jane umbrella stroller, which has a reclining seat for very young babies, a foot rest, and vinyl hood and is available at local baby retail outlets for about $100.
- A baby (front) pack for small babies. The luxury front pack is the Snugli model with dacron and cotton for easy washing or hot climates. It is available at local baby retail outlets for about $55.
- A baby/child back carrier. The "Gerry" (Gerico) Frame Carrier has a head support, padded back support, and bottle and accessory carrier case and is available at local outlets for about $50.
- A baby carrier/seat/car seat. For a car or airplane safety seat that doubles as a portable baby seat/carrier bed, the "Gerry" (Gerico) Guardian car seat has an adjustable chest protector and washable cushion, as well as an accessory compartment, and is available at local outlets for about $80. A less expensive alternative, without the car safety feature, is the Century "Kanga Rockaroo" infant carrier with a washable cloth cover, brace, and handle carrier and a plastic bottle pouch. It is available at local outlets for about $50.
- Customary food and containers (jars of strained foods, cereals, or crackers so that you do not have to depend on strange airline meals or serving hours)
- Disposable diapers
- A container of wet wipes
- Zinc oxide or other diaper rash ointment
- Tear-free shampoo
- A warm cover for air-conditioned areas
- The child's special teddy bear and/or security blanket
- For older children, a large pad, pencils, and a separate box of

crayons for each child, a favorite book, a tape deck with favorite tapes

2.18   Children on tour are great ice-breakers. Their needs and their charm are universal—even a Communist dialectical imperative will melt before the cry of a child who needs a diaper change. A book on traveling with children that has received rave reviews from all quarters is *Fielding's Europe with Children,* by Leila Hadley (1984), published by William Morrow and Company, Blue Guides, 105 Madison Avenue, New York, NY 10018. It is available at most bookstores that carry travel publications for about $13. (See also 1.14, Travel Documents; 1.77, Reaction to Shots; 1.84, Power of Attorney; 1.130, Will Should Appoint Guardian.)

Luggage and Apparel

Luggage

2.19   From the standpoint of convenience and personal safety, it is best to fit all you plan to carry in one large suitcase (to be checked on board) and one carry-on bag that has a shoulder strap. This allows you to carry all your luggage yourself if need be; and with a shoulder strap on your carry-on bag, one hand will be free to handle documents or to push through a crowd (or to ward off hucksters).

2.20   For executives who want to carry briefcases, some carry-on bags with shoulder straps can accommodate a briefcase inside and still fit under the airplane seat. Carrying a briefcase inside the carry-on bag leaves one hand free of encumbrances (and conceals businesslike luggage from skyjackers). Carry-on luggage can also accommodate a purse—although a woman might consider wearing a waist purse on a belt around the waist or across the body from one shoulder to the other. (For other secure carrying devices, see 2.11.)

2.21   Fancy, expensive-looking luggage is inconsistent with good personal security. Such luggage is an immediate eye catcher for anyone trying to find the the flushest pocket to pick. Soft luggage (for example, nylon vinyl collapsible luggage) is less conspicuous than rigid, new-looking aluminum or pastel plastic luggage.

2.22 Put sturdy tags on the outside and inside of all luggage so that lost luggage can be identified and returned to you. You may wish to put a strip of tape on the outside of your luggage so that you can readily spot it at the baggage claim area. If you want to avoid being identified by onlookers who may read your luggage tags, you can make a snug envelope for the tag by doubling over a piece of note paper and wrapping the paper around the tag with tape. The envelope will be open at both ends and can be slipped off easily to read the tag. It is both practical and secure to use your office address on luggage tags so that any calls regarding lost luggage will not come to your home in your absence.

Clothing

2.23 The appropriate clothing to take with you depends on so many variables—including the weather—that it is beyond the scope of this guide. Before you travel, you should certainly ask your customer/client/host what is necessary and suitable for the season and local custom.

2.24 The following are clothing suggestions for men:

- Take suits with pants that can also be used separately as slacks. If you have a suit with two pairs of pants, one pair will stay pressed for use after work.
- Some suit coats may also serve as sports coats with slacks, thus avoiding the need for an extra sports jacket. A suitable combination might be gray flannel pants and a navy blue or dark green suit jacket.
- If you have the hotel dry cleaners clean your suits, you may need no more than two suits even for an extended visit.
- Try to travel with only two pairs of shoes, since they are heavy and bulky. Wear the most comfortable pair in flight. One pair of black shoes can do for business wear during the day and formal wear at night. Also take Japanese sandals for hotel or beach use;

a common tourist injury is stubbed or broken toes caused by walking barefoot in the dark in hotel rooms (see also 1.68).

- Take an extra shirt in your hand luggage in case your suitcase is lost or delayed.
- Pack a sweater or windbreaker in your hand luggage, even in summer, for use on the air-conditioned plane.
- Take a light topcoat in case of rainy weather. Also, depending on the time of year and the climate, you may need warmer or more weather-resistant outer wear.
- Take tennis shoes or heavy-duty boots if you will need them, since many countries do not have standard sizes large enough for American feet.

2.25   The following are clothing suggestions for women:

- Take a basic business or "weekender" wardrobe, such as a tailored jacket and matching skirt and blouse and a coordinated skirt and blouse or sweater. Your emphasis should be on textures and colors that are interchangeable.
- Take three pairs of shoes—one set of dressy shoes and two sets of low-heeled walking shoes (the extra set for when one pair gets wet or muddy). Wear comfortable walking shoes on the airplane. Also take Japanese sandals for the hotel or beach, and take tennis shoes or boots if you expect to need them, since foreign stores may not carry your size.
- Take an extra blouse in your hand luggage in case your suitcase is lost or delayed.
- If you use the hotel dry cleaners, you won't need to have a lot of extra clothing.
- Pack a light sweater in your hand luggage, even in summer, for use on the air-conditioned plane.
- Take a light topcoat in case of rainy weather and, if necessary, a warmer or more weather-resistant coat.

Advance Shipment by Courier

2.26   If you have extensive time to plan a business trip, it may be possible to send bulky materials—such as catalogues and sales brochures—in advance, by courier, so that they are at your destination when you arrive. This also may be a safety consideration. If you are an arms salesman, for example, you may not want to have sales brochures with you if a terrorist should take over the flight.

What to Wear on the Plane

2.27 For the trip itself, a male traveler may wish to wear a dark-colored older suit, perhaps drip-dry and certainly wrinkle-resistant. Such a suit would be acceptable in case you have to proceed directly to a business meeting when you arrive abroad. Sports clothes make you look more like a tourist, however, and thus may be more secure, but don't appear too scruffy, or you may get an additional search by airport security.

2.28 Especially if she is being met, a businesswoman may also wish to wear a suit. Dark colors and prints show less sign of travel.

2.29 Air safety specialists at the National Transportation Safety Board (NTSB) say that pure wool and cotton clothes are better protection against heat and fire in an air crash. Synthetic-fiber clothes will melt when exposed to heat and fire, and you are thus more likely to be injured. If safety is your highest priority, use pure, natural-fiber clothing for travel (see also 3.14).

What You Should Carry on Your Person or Have Readily Accessible in Your Hand Luggage

Pocket or Purse Items

2.30 The following items should be carried in your pocket or purse for easy accessibility:

- Your airline ticket
- Your passport. After boarding the plane, put your passport in your hand luggage to delay its presentation to terrorists. If you

carry more than one passport, such as an official and a tourist passport, make sure that any terrorist search will produce the tourist passport or the passport of the nationality of least risk first (see also 3.20).

- Your driver's license. If you plan to rent a car, also have your AAA card or international permit (see 1.17 and 1.18).
- Your health insurance card
- Enough U.S. dollars to pay for the cab to the airport, reading material or a meal at the airport, any overweight luggage charges at the ticket counter, and any drinks in flight
- A small amount of foreign currency (see 1.23) or small-denomination U.S. dollars (see 1.26)—enough to get you to your hotel when you arrive at your destination
- Your vaccination record (generally no longer required, except where indicated for special conditions)
- Some of your traveler's checks
- One or two credit cards (such as your telephone credit card)
- Keys to the bags you are going to check
- Your daily schedule/notebook/address book
- Your airline VIP club card (if you are a member)
- Any hotel discount cards (such as Continental Club)

2.31   Opinions and styles differ on what is a "must" for ready access. Many items that are usually carried in a wallet or purse—gasoline credit cards, library card, office ID, membership cards, house keys, office keys—may be left at home. Also a wallet with credit cards and cash in it is an easier target for a pickpocket than separate items carried in various pockets. It is best not to carry items in your hip pockets, which are the most easily picked. Jacket or coat breast pockets are also a security risk. If you remove your jacket during the flight and put it in an overhead rack, items may fall out of the pocket or be stolen while you sleep. This risk may be minimized by having a loop and button sewn into your jacket to secure the breast pocket. For men, front pants pockets, though inconvenient for access, are the most secure places to carry items on your person.

2.32 Don't wear valuable jewelry or an expensive-looking watch. They make you an obvious target for thievery when you arrive overseas.

Securing Your Money and Valuables

2.33 Divide your large-denomination traveler's checks and cash between your hand luggage and a money belt or money carrier, so that if your luggage is lost or your pocket is picked, you will lose only part of your funds. You can put these large-denomination bills and traveler's checks in inaccessible places, since you will usually need only small bills until you are at the hotel or have at least left the airport. If you are carrying two currencies, you might avoid confusion by putting each currency in a different place.

How to Pack Your Hand Luggage in Anticipation of Your Needs on the Day of Departure

2.34 The sequence of your needs on the day of departure is as follows:

- Your airline ticket and passport for boarding
- In-flight items (reading materials, work materials)
- Your passport and customs declaration for disembarking
- Your passport if you wish to buy local currency at the destination airport
- Your ticket and passport to confirm your return flight at the destination airport
- Local currency or small-denomination U.S. currency for porters, snacks, and cab fare to the hotel

Seasoned travelers establish a routine for carrying necessary items in accessible and secure places and putting them back in the same places.

2.35 At the top of your hand luggage, or readily accessible, should be your toilet articles, medicines, and survival items—all of which should fit into a vanity case or plastic bag. These items should include a fire and smoke escape mask as described in 2.12, Emergency Items and 3.18, Smoke Masks. You should also have a light sweater handy for use on the air-conditioned plane.

It will be convenient to be able to reach a prepackaged, moist towelette, a handkerchief or paper napkin for spills, a zip-lock bag for unexpected leaky items, a shoehorn, and anything you brought to eat on board without having to rummage through your hand luggage. If you are a shutter bug, you also may want to have your camera within reach.

2.36 If you plan to work during the flight, you should organize your briefcase or carry-on bag so that your work items are on top, not buried deep in the bag.

2.37 Such advance planning may seem obvious, but remember that when you have traveled far, you are likely to be slightly disoriented when you arrive and have to deal with a foreign language. Keep as many aspects of your trip as routine and free of aggravation as possible, so that your energies can be saved for unexpected crises—not spent on a mislaid passport. Maintain routine procedures throughout your trip, such as having a standard place for your watch, glasses, and other necessities when you go to bed in the hotel or when you go to the beach.

3
Safe Travel: Preflight and In-Flight Tips

At the Ticket Counter

Checking Your Luggage

3.1 Keep your luggage together in sight. When you are at the counter negotiating with the airline attendant, put your hand luggage on the floor beside your foot so that it is touching your foot or leg during the conversation. This is especially important in the frenzy of foreign airports, where lines may be replaced by free-for-alls. A family or group may wish to put tape and numbers on the luggage, so that it can be accounted for quickly when unloading or loading.

3.2 Watch the luggage you are checking on board until you see that it has baggage tickets attached to it and that the stubs have been stapled to your ticket cover. You should have luggage tags on all bags you are not carrying by hand; and attach identification, such as a business card, inside the bag in case the tags are lost. Bright-colored luggage straps help keep roughly handled luggage from breaking open and will help you identify your luggage on arrival.

3.3 If your luggage has any detachable pieces, such as a backpack frame or carrier, make sure that each piece has identification tags and that they are attached securely. You may want a separate baggage ticket for each detachable part of the luggage.

3.4 Locking your luggage is a good precaution against pilfering and against the bags opening by mistake, as well as minimal protection if the airlines misroute or lose your luggage. If you are not good at locating small keys, use a combination or digital travel lock. A combination lock or a digital travel lock is available from the Hoffritz catalogue, 1-800-962-9639, for about $15.

Note: In mainland China and some other countries, only locked luggage may be checked on board.

3.5 If you are late checking your luggage or arrive at the last minute before flight time, make sure that your checked luggage will travel on the same flight you are traveling on, so that you don't have to wait around an airport for the next flight some hours later—or even the next day. If no guarantee can be given, see if the bags can be hand-carried and stowed on board.

Because of close timing between connecting flights in New York or some other major air hub, your luggage may not be put on your flight. It may be better to collect your luggage and hand-carry it to your connecting flight. (For overseas flights at most international airports, new security requirements now dictate that you must appear at the counter with all luggage to board the plane.)

Presenting Your Ticket

3.6 After you have presented your ticket and documents at the airline counter, make sure that you place them in a safe but accessible place for quick use on disembarkation. Bear in mind that a professional thief at the airport will have observed where you placed these items, so put them in a pocket with a button or a pouch with a zipper closing.

3.7 Check that your ticket has the correct number of coupons left in it and that the attendant did not inadvertently pull two out.

In Flight

The Safest Seats During Crashes, Fires, and Terrorist Incidents

3.8 National Transportation Safety Board (NTSB) specialists and many flight attendants say that rear seats are safer for surviving initial impact in an airplane crash. After the crash, however, quick evacuation to escape smoke and fire—the worst killer in air crashes—is paramount. A fire—usually caused by ignited fuel escaping from one of the wing fuel tanks—is likely to block exits on one side of the downed plane and, within a few seconds, can melt the plastic windows and spread smoke and fire inside the plane. NTSB specialists and flight attendants recommend sitting in an aisle seat, away from a window, that gives you quick access to exits on both sides (and the rear) of the plane (see also 3.11–3.18.)

3.9 Terrorist hijackers will be most likely to focus their initial efforts on the cockpit of an aircraft, as in the June 1985 hijacking of TWA Flight 874 from Athens and the September 1986 hijacking of Pan Am Flight 73 from Karachi. The focus was still on the cockpit when the shooting started in Karachi. Those seated away from the aisle, farthest from the terrorists' regular patrols, received less abuse than those sitting in aisle seats in both incidents. In these two recent incidents, the best seat was a seat in the back of the plane, near an exit—not an aisle seat.

Some security advisors say that the safest seats during a terrorist hijacking are over-the-wing window seats in the mid to aft section of the plane, near the egress to the wing for an escape route. These seats are far from the cockpit—where terrorist activities start—and far from the rear and front exits—where the first rescue attack might start (for example, the Egyptian commando high-fire-power assault on the hijacked Egyptian flight grounded in Malta in November 1985). A countervailing consideration is that the most certain danger point is the initial show of terrorist force at the pilot's cabin door and subsequent abuse of those in aisle seats; you want to be as far away from that activity or later activity at the cabin command post as possible. Also, there is no certainty of a rescue attempt. Thus, rear window seats near an exit are safest from hijackers. Note, too, that in the September 1986 Pan Am hijacking, the passengers who escaped via fore and aft escape chutes suffered fewer injuries than those who jumped from the wing to the hard tarmac. It is also noteworthy that aft (and fore) air escape chutes form into floating life rafts for accidents at sea, while wing exits don't have direct access to life rafts.

A Note of Caution: If you are a robust and vigorous-looking male traveler, terrorists who take command of an airplane are likely to move you from a seat next to an exit in the rear (or front) and make you the target of attention and abuse. If you fit this description, try to sit in a window seat near the rear, one or two aisles from the exit aisle, or in a seat near the center of the exit aisle.

3.10   Despite the foregoing safety factors, there are advantages to sitting in the front of the plane, including ease of disembarkation and no smoking. Sitting in the no-smoking section may be important on foreign airlines, where people tend to smoke more and where IATA regulations may not be so strictly enforced. Also, aisle seats give ready access to facilities and allow you to get up and walk around without disturbing others.

Emergency Crash Landing and Evacuation Procedures

3.11   At the beginning of your flight, listen carefully to the flight attendant's safety instructions, and review the routes to the exits near you and the instructions for opening the airplane door.

3.12   If your flight is over water, see that there is a life jacket under your seat and review the steps for putting on the life jacket, getting out of the plane at sea, and inflating your life jacket. Watch the flight attendant's demonstration, and look at the instruction card.

3.13   Review in your mind how you would get to each nearby exit if the plane were filled with smoke and all around you were in panic (see also 2.12 and 3.18).

3.14 If a crash seems imminent and you have a wool overcoat (remember that synthetic-fiber materials will melt in heat and fire, injuring you), put the coat on to act as a block against heat and fire.

3.15 If a crash seems imminent, put on shoes as foot protection against bruises on impact and against heat and fire—even though you are instructed to take them off. Don't wear heeled shoes, however, which will make you unstable if you must find your way through smoke and may harm the escape slide.

3.16 If a crash seems imminent, tighten your seat belt around your hips as tight as possible, brace your feet on the leg frame of the seat in front of you, double up so that your head is on your knees, and cradle your head in your arms for skull protection.

3.17 If there is smoke after the landing, breathe as little as possible and crawl below the smoke to the exit by the path you have reviewed beforehand. If you have a smoke mask, put it on (see 2.12 and 3.18).

3.18 The suggestions given here are a combination of advice from airline personnel and recommendations in "Air Safety: The Shocking Truth," by David Noland, in the October 1986 issue of *Discover* magazine. The article also advises travelers to carry the Sheldahl Aviation Oxygen Escape Breathing Device, which gives the wearer from two to eight minutes of extra breathing time in a cabin filled with smoke. A spokesman for the Sheldahl Corporation (Northfield, Minnesota) says that current product liability laws and litigation prevent the company from manufacturing their patented product and from licensing any other manufacturer, worldwide, to make it. At present, there is a fire and smoke escape mask marketed under the brand name Vivat in Europe, sold through Woodville Polymer Engineering, Ltd., Staffordshire, U.K., Attn: Peter Shrubsall. Call 283-22-11-22. A modification of this product will be sold in the United States in 1988. Inquiries should be addressed to Intech, 6611 Waterwood Trail, Fort Worth, TX 76132, 817-731-2915. This clear plastic hood slips over the head and has a passive filter placed in front of the wearer's mouth. The unit comes in a sealed plastic case measuring 5½" x 8" and weighs less than five ounces. This product is a must for frequent air travelers and for those who want additional protection from smoke in hotels or office buildings.

Note: The definitive work on airplane safety, according to the International Airline Passenger Association (IAPA) of Dallas, Texas, is *Just in Case: A Passenger Guide to Airplane Safety and Survival* by Danie Johnson (1984), Plenum Press, 233 Spring St., New York, NY 10013, for about $20. Also available by mail or by calling the public relations office of the National Transportation Safety Board (NTSB) in Washington, DC (202-382-6600) are annual safety records of airlines and individual commercial aircraft, identified by tail number. These reports are kept by the Safety Programs Office of the NTSB.

What to Do During a Terrorist Hijacking

3.19 The 1985 TWA hijacking in Athens and the 1986 Pan Am hijacking in Karachi show that the first move of terrorists after securing an airplane is to single out Americans—especially American government or military personnel and Jewish Americans—for rough treatment or execution, to convince authorities that further violence will result if terrorist demands are not met. (In Karachi, British citizens were second on the hit list after Americans.)

3.20 The terrorists' first step will be to demand the passengers' passports. If you carry an American (or British or, perhaps, French) passport, your goal is to delay presentation of your passport as long as possible.

One way to stall for time is to keep your passport in your hand luggage or in a coat pocket in the overhead compartment, so that if the terrorists force you to move from your seat, you will not have your passport with you.

If the hijacking endures for long, however—as in the TWA flight from Athens in 1985—you will eventually have to produce your passport. With luck, the initial demonstration of force will be over by that time.

Note: The American media—with apparent disregard for the

safety of American travelers in possible future terrorist skyjackings—exposed the fact that the Pan Am Flight 73 hostess in Karachi thwarted the terrorists' attempt to find Americans by not collecting their passports or by disposing of the few she did collect. In the next skyjacking, the terrorists are likely to collect the passports themselves at gunpoint.

Disembarking

Presenting Your Documents

3.21 When you arrive at your destination, have your passport, visas, and filled-out customs declaration ready for presentation—not buried deep in your hand luggage. Have your doctor's certificate ready with your medicine kit in case it is required.

3.22 It is important that you find out whether any documents given to you on entry, such as currency-exchange documents, must be presented on departure; ask a flight attendant or immigration official. If these documents must be kept, stow them with your other travel documents.

3.23 If security or customs authorities ask the purpose of your trip, answer "pleasure" unless you have a business visa or some other visa that will require more explanation (see also 1.10 and 1.11).

Clearing Customs

3.24 It is best not to be the very first or the very last to go through customs in a country where you do not know the ropes. Having others precede you at customs enables you to see what is being looked for, how extensively your luggage is going to be searched, and whether one line is moving faster or one customs agent seems to be in a better mood than another. If you are last at customs, there will be no other travelers behind you to see what is going on, and you may be alone with the customs official.

3.25 If it becomes apparent, by an overly thorough search of your luggage or by direct request, that some favor is in order, there are some obvious steps to take, as well as some evasive tactics. First, play dumb; do not display your linguistic abilities (if you have any). At some point, the official may suggest an acceptable "resolution." Remember, however, that bribes are illegal and are frowned upon by most European and U.S. customs officials.

If time is not an issue and you are a risk-taker, you can show your outrage and make a row by calling for the police or asking to call your embassy. If this tactic seems to work, it is usually prudent not to persist after the official has backed off. Who knows—you may have to deal with that official again someday. The best tactic of all is to stick to the law.

Reporting Lost Luggage

3.26 When you report lost luggage to the airline, the attendant will ask for your baggage ticket. Write down all the numbers and information on the baggage ticket, so that you will have an independent record of these details—or, if possible, keep the ticket and have the airline attendant write down the details. This ticket is your only evidence that you checked the bag with the airline and your only way of tracing it. At the very least, get a written receipt from the airport attendant.

The International Airline Passengers Association (IAPA) offers a lost luggage retrieval service as part of its standard membership. A call to an IAPA worldwide service center will often save your having to hound the offending airline. Information about IAPA is available by calling Dallas, Texas 214-520-1070 or 1-800-527-8888 (see also note following 1.54). The annual membership fee is about $90.

4
Arrival on Foreign Soil

From Customs to Your Hotel: A Risky Period

The First Moments

4.1 As you walk through the door from customs to the airport concourse, you may be carrying a suitcase in one hand and your carry-on luggage by its shoulder strap. If the flight has been a crowded one to a major city, there will probably be throngs of people to greet the passengers on the flight. Before you can find a porter or the person who is meeting you, you will have to be in the middle of that jostling crowd. At that moment, it is best to have your documents and money in a safe pocket or a zipped compartment of your carry-on bag. Some additional precautions you might take include trying to leave one hand free, so that you can react to jostling and get through the crowd, and putting your wristwatch on your right hand, where a pickpocket would not expect it to be, or putting it in your pocket until you are in a cab or in your hotel.

4.2 Many modern metropolitan airports—de Gaulle airport in Paris, for example—provide luggage pushcarts for disembarking passengers that may be used to the point where you can board a taxi. The availability of such pushcarts, plus the additional police security in the wake of increased terrorist activity, have reduced the risks for arriving air travelers. In many countries, however, airport pushcarts may be used only to the exit door of the customs area. In these countries, the risk for arriving travelers from the jostling crowd remains a security consideration.

Exchanging Currency upon Arrival

4.3 If you will need local currency for a taxi to your hotel, there is likely to be some facility for money exchange at the airport. In some countries, it is mandatory that you exchange a minimum amount of dollars, and some do not allow you to bring local currency with you (see also 1.23–1.26).

Note: The exchange rate at the airport is likely to be an unfavorable one. In general, exchange the least amount necessary to serve your immediate needs or to comply with local regulation. Remember to ask for small denominations of bills or for coins so that you can pay for the taxi or bus in exact change. Ask the person at the exchange counter how much the cab fare to your hotel should cost, so that you can buy the proper amount—and defend yourself against overcharging by the cab.

4.4 When you leave the counter of the foreign exchange window, remember that any interested observer will have seen where you put your passport and your money. Be sure to put them in a safe place.

4.5 In some Latin American countries, it is common for people to offer informal exchanges of foreign currency at the airport. Such people also may offer to find you a cab or to carry your luggage. It is best to keep moving and to avoid conversation with anyone making such offers. A more favorable exchange rate is not worth the risk of exposure to a professional pickpocket or arrest for an illegal currency exchange transaction.

Confirming Your Return Flight

4.6 In major cities, you needn't worry about confirming your return flight at the airport; your hotel can take care of such matters. In small cities or out-of-the-way places, however, it is practical to confirm your departure flight as you arrive. Confirming it later may require a long wait at some air office across town from your hotel. Many airlines require that you reconfirm your flight within twenty-four hours of the flight. As you confirm the return flight on arrival, ask about such reconfirmation requirements and observe them.

Some airlines automatically bump travelers who fail to reconfirm and charge them an additional fare.

Being Met at the Airport

4.7 If you are being met at the airport by someone you know, everything should go smoothly, and your security worries should be over. You should, however, have the telephone number and address—for both work hours and after-hours—of those who are meeting you. Planes are often delayed and may arrive at inconvenient hours, and there may be no way to contact in advance the person who is supposed to meet you. It can be very unpleasant to arrive in Rio de Janeiro in the early hours of the morning—when the flight was scheduled to arrive at midday—and have to locate the right José de Souza (John Smith) in the phone book.

4.8 If you are being met by a stranger, be sure that you have a clear plan for getting together. You might not want a driver or company officer standing in the reception area holding a large sign with your name or company on it. (In some Latin American countries in the 1970s, kidnappings of business executives were engineered by having supposed company limousines meet the target executive.) In any case, you should have some description whereby you can recognize the person who is there to meet you—a physical description of the person or of something the person will be carrying, such as a company brochure. Again, you should have a phone number for contacting the person during office hours and after-hours. You should also know where you are going to stay, so that you can get there by yourself if necessary.

Getting from the Airport to Your Hotel on Your Own

4.9 Being "taken for a ride" the long way by taxicabs is a universal expectation in Third World countries (and even in some First World countries). Your best defense is to ask a policeman or a foreign exchange dealer to tell you what the price should be and to get a firm price quotation from your driver before you start. Also ask if there is a separate fee for luggage. Be sure you know enough about the local currency to identify the bill you should use for payment. Often, new currency will confuse everyone but the cabbie.

Other defenses against being "taken for a ride" are (1) using a prepaid airport limousine service, so that you must pay only the tip when you arrive at the hotel; (2) having the hotel doorman pay the taxi driver and reimbursing him; or, (3) paying in small-denomination U.S. currency. It the taxi driver refuses the U.S. currency, get change in the hotel and ask the doorman to negotiate the amount of the fare. Never accept an airport taxi driver's invitation to go on a sight-seeing tour on the way to the hotel— unless you do not mind being taken.

4.10   In remote areas, it is best to see the vehicle in which you will ride before making any commitments. Since you are likely to have a speedy ride, pick the largest and safest-looking vehicle at the taxi stand.

4.11   Sharp business practices aside, taxi drivers are often good sources of information about local politics, museums, sporting events, restaurants, and extracurricular entertainment. They are often authorities on where it is safe for foreigners to walk alone at night (or find attractive company), what neighborhoods to avoid, and what hazards may be near your hotel. For most taxi drivers, foreign languages do not seem to be a barrier to communication on such matters.

Arrival at Your Hotel: First Steps

Fire Safety

4.12   Your first security consideration at the hotel is how to get out in case of fire or other disaster. When you are being led to your room by the bellhop, make sure that it is not at the end of a long hall in an isolated wing with no exit. Unless the hotel is filled to capacity, few desk clerks will refuse to make a room change if you start a loud discussion about fire hazards in the hotel. Some cautious travelers always book hotel rooms below the fifth floor—within reach of a fire ladder.

4.13 When you leave the room for the first time, follow the exit signs and go down the stairs all the way to the lobby, so that you will know whether there are any bottlenecks or unusual turns—or even a locked door where there shouldn't be. You may wish to repeat this trip on your second departure from your room. Remember that if there is a fire at night, halls and stairways may be dark, and there may be smoke and panic-stricken people around you. You should memorize the way to the exit: How many doorways to the exit from my room? Where is the handrail to the stairs? Make sure that you can easily grab your hotel room key at night, so that you can get back into your room in case you cannot escape by the stairs. Such attention to detail, even when you are tired after a long journey and late to a meeting, may save your life.

Note: As the disastrous New Year's Eve 1986 fire at the duPont Hotel in Puerto Rico showed, it may be vital that you know both the fire exit *down* the stairs and the exit *up* the stairs to the roof. You may not research the details of this exit immediately, but it will be critical information if it is needed.

Room Security

4.14 You don't want unexpected visitors in your hotel room. When you first arrive in your room, make sure that none of the windows are readily accessible from the street, and be sure that windows and balcony doors are locked. See that they are also locked whenever you leave the room and at night. Standard urban precautions apply: keep your door locked at all times, and identify any visitors before you open the door.

Telephones and Telephone Communications

4.15 Once you have checked in to your hotel, you will want to make any necessary calls and set up your appointments. This is also a chance to confirm that your emergency telephone numbers for the U.S. Embassy and American Express (or other traveler's check issuers) are correct (for example, that the prefix code number has not been changed).

4.16   If you are traveling with others, including family, make sure that they know how and where to reach you by phone and in person and that they have emergency telephone numbers to call. Also give them a foreign introductory phrase to use on the phone in trying to contact you or in an emergency. (Review your code communications from 1.131.)

4.17   When you leave for your first meeting, it would be prudent to stop in the hotel lobby and practice the procedures for using a public telephone. In some countries, public telephones require a slug instead of a coin. You should buy four or five slugs at the hotel desk to carry in your pocket—or have a few coins in your pocket for using in a public phone.

4.18   Telephones in most developed countries work efficiently, but those in Third World countries often do not. It may take several minutes to get a dial tone, overloaded circuits make connections on the first attempt rare, connections may be poor during rainstorms, and many homes and offices may not have telephones. Plan any meetings ahead of time; do not depend on the telephone for confirming appointments, especially in countries where the telephone service is known to be uncertain.

4.19   In general, you should not consider the telephones in your hotel as "secure" for discussions of sensitive business or personal matters.

4.20   Most hotels place a high surcharge on overseas calls. To avoid these high charges, you may wish to call your home collect and ask them to call you back.

Local Transportation

4.21   Get a subway map from the hotel desk or from your city guide and determine how well the subway can serve your transportation needs. If your hotel is centrally located and many of the offices where your meetings will be held are in a central business district, the subway can be one of the most secure means of travel. You may not even have to go outside your hotel to get to the subway entrance (so any surveillant would have to be observing you in the lobby), and you may arrive only steps from your destination. The security precautions detailed in 5.3–5.23 and 5.43–5.54 also apply to subway travel. There is no better cure for rush hour, however, than the Paris (or London or Buenos Aires) subway.

4.22 If the subway requires a token, buy some in advance and keep them in your pocket. Some new systems require a two-way ticket with a magnetic strip; buy some in advance.

Choosing a Taxi

4.23 Security advisors disagree about whether you should take a cab from the hotel cab line or walk down the street to hail a cab. You want a cab that cannot be rigged with a terrorist or his ally as the driver. If you see that the hotel doorman is selecting cabs out of the line, or that the taxi drivers have some say in who they take, then you should be wary of taxi-stand cabs. If the line is clearly first-come, first-served and the pace is brisk, then the risk is slight.

4.24 An alternative is to have the hotel desk call a cab for you. This is certain to be secure if you are in a small hotel where the desk clerks are well known to the management. These clerks are likely to become helpful allies once you have been in the hotel for a few days.

Registering at the U.S. Embassy

4.25 In a trouble spot or in a country with potential problems (such as earthquake-prone Mexico) registering at the U.S. Embassy is a must, so that the embassy can contact you or help locate you in the rubble if a problem develops. If you plan an extended stay anywhere, registration if a good precaution. However, you must appear at the embassy or consulate in person to register, so if your visit is short, your schedule is heavy, the incidence of crime and terrorism is low, and you are not on an earthquake fault line, you can skip it.

5

Daily Security Planning for Business or Pleasure

Reviewing Potential Security Problems: Street Crime, Terrorism, and Hostile Governments

5.1 Based on your pretravel investigations into security problems in the country you are visiting (see 1.87 and 1.88), you should have some idea of what dangers to expect. If not, your first precaution should be to ask your local customer/client/host or a U.S. Embassy officer about the following points:

- The local street crime problem and how it affects foreign visitors
- The source, size, method of operation, and target of any terrorist activity and how it may affect U.S. business and foreign visitors
- The attitude of the host government toward foreign business in general and toward your business and your company in particular, as well as toward American tourists.

In reviewing these security problems, you should bear in mind that, in the case of street crime, you are trying to thwart a general, untargeted threat that is aimed at anyone, but particularly at unwary foreigners. By contrast, in the case of a terrorist threat, you are trying to thwart a finely targeted threat to injure or kidnap a specific business representative or group, to embarrass the local government and serve political objectives. Likewise, unfavorable attention of the host government is a problem specific to your business or company. These distinctions are important when you are plotting your defenses.

Street Crime: Thwarting Theft and Assault

5.2   Most travelers who have been assaulted and robbed on the street have done something to show their vulnerability to their assailant. They have dressed so that they are conspicuous as foreign tourists; they have been alone on foot in crowded shopping areas; they have loaded themselves down with purchases in bulky bags; they have been inattentive to how they carried their purse or wallet; they have walked casually, without observing people in the crowd around them; or they have worn jewelry or a valuable watch. Thus, they have made themselves targets. There are several standard dos and don'ts which can eliminate such vulnerability and reduce the risk of theft and assault.

Dos and Don'ts for Walking in Public Places

5.3   Don't wear conspicuous clothing. If everyone on the street is wearing dark, formal clothing and you wear white shorts and a Hawaiian sports shirt, or a pink drip-dry suit, you will attract the eye of a potential street thief.

5.4   Don't wear jewelry—even a wedding ring—or a valuable watch in public. Don't wear fake jewelry that looks real. Put your watch in your pocket or use a cheap watch—and wear it on your right wrist. If jewelry or your bar of decorations is required for a formal evening, hide them under a topcoat or put them in your pocket until you have arrived.

5.5   Don't carry your passport unless you need it. Passports are a common target for street thieves. Carry your International Driver's Permit and a photocopy of your passport, unless some anticipated transaction may require a passport. If you take your passport, put it in a pouch under your clothing or in a secure, buttoned inner pocket. If you don't carry your passport, make sure the document you do carry includes your emergency telephone numbers and blood type information.

5.6 Don't walk aimlessly or alone in crowded public places. A brisk pace implies a set destination. Walking with others will intimidate a prospective assailant.

5.7 Avoid street vendors and crowds, especially groups of children, in the street. The standard technique for picking pockets or slitting purses or bags is for a street vendor or child to approach you as if to make a sale. While you are focused on the object and the unintelligible spiel, you are surrounded by other children who encourage you to make the purchase. Deft hands rifle your pockets or slit the underside of your bag with a razor. Similarly, don't take a shoeshine in the open street, and be careful about giving handouts to street urchins, especially if it requires that you take out your wallet or stoop down while other kids are around you. Another pickpocketing approach is for a street vendor to spill something on your clothes "accidentally" and help clean it off—by cleaning you out. Anticipate that someone who bumps into you on the street may be stalling you for a friend who is walking just behind you. Don't stop to talk; just keep walking, away from the vendor or crowd. If possible, dodge into a store off the street, or hail a cab. If you are confronted by two or three men in your path and retreat is impossible, walk forward, pushing (straight-arming) one man out of the way, and say, "I am in a hurry and can't stop." Just keep moving at a firm pace.

5.8 Don't load yourself down with a bag full of purchases that must be carried some distance in crowded streets or on the subway. This makes you easy prey, because you will be walking slowly and will have your hands full—as well as being conspicuous. Buy in small, easily carried bundles, or take a cab—or have things delivered to your hotel. Fancier stores may, for an additional charge, package and send your purchases to you in the United States.

5.9 Don't invite danger by going to high-risk places such as slums or off-the-beaten-track bars or to strangers' apartments. In Bogotá in the late 1970s, a standard assault tactic on a main street near a well-known slum was for two assailants to approach a lone tourist in the street from two directions. One would stab the tourist's bare wrist with a knife while the other tore the watch from the other wrist. Police would not venture into the slum. Well-known, established nightclubs and brothels maintain their reputation by having thorough screening and tough bouncers; risks there are of a different kind. If you are interested in prostitutes, don't look in lonely side streets, and don't accept an invitation to go to a hotel or apartment that the prostitute suggests. Go to a well-known "house," find her in well-lit surroundings (perhaps through the front desk), and take her to your room or to a place you have arranged beforehand, where *you* have control of the situation and she cannot signal her friends.

5.10 Don't try to be brave in the face of danger—run away and yell for help. If you are hit or stabbed, stay on the ground; don't invite further punishment. Your life and health are worth more than your possessions.

5.11 Do put your documents, wallet, money, and any valuables that you must carry in a shoulder-strap pouch, a money belt, an inside pocket with a button, or a purse that can be carried like a football. This thwarts pickpockets, even in a crowd. You should carry some money or a wallet with some money in it in your pocket, so that if you are held up, a hasty thief will be satisfied without getting to your real valuables.

5.12 Carry only the documents, cash, and credit cards you need. If you are walking to a nearby restaurant for dinner, carry only one credit card, some cash, and a photocopy of your passport. Leave your passport and other valuables in a safe place at the hotel. For small purchases, pin a few small bills inside your pocket (especially women with large skirt pockets).

5.13 Do make sure that someone knows where you are going and when you expect to return, so that you will be missed if something happens to you. Telephone ahead that you are on your way to an appointment.

5.14 Before walking into the street from your hotel or office, look around at people loitering in the street—both men and women. Observe their facial and clothing details, so you would recognize them if you saw them again later in the day. Look at hair color and shoes especially, since they are not readily changed. This is a precaution against both street crime and stakeout surveillance by terrorists. The street criminal is likely to focus on alternative candidates if you have obviously looked over the loiterers, if you don't appear to be wearing any valuables, and if you walk briskly, as if to a known destination (see also 5.27). Be especially alert near the American Express office, the U.S. Embassy, and other places where Americans congregate.

5.15 Do get a street map, and get directions at the hotel desk, before going on a shopping expedition or walking to an appointment. Know where you are going to make your purchases. If you get lost, go into a store off the street, with your map, to ask further directions. This will allow you to walk at a brisk pace and will prevent vendors or kids from delaying your progress. Remember to ask if there are any particular areas or routes that should be avoided.

5.16 Do get a subway map and learn the subway system. The subway is usually secure at busy times of day, but beware of the jostling crowd. Have your valuables in a secure place, inside a buttoned pocket or in a pouch. Also, beware of drunks or kids who might be acting as a diversion for the pickpocket standing next to you.

5.17 Do your shopping with a group, or get someone from your customer/client/host's office to go with you. There is safety in numbers, and it is especially useful to have a guide who is alert to local dangers.

5.18 Walk on the street side of the sidewalk, away from the building line. Stay in well-lit areas. If the sidewalk is narrow, walk in the street facing oncoming traffic. Carry your purse or tote bag on the shoulder away from the street. Avoid "choke points," such as between a newspaper kiosk and a building that might conceal an attacker, by crossing the street. If you feel fearful, hail a cab and go to your hotel.

5.19 Always look in both directions before crossing a street. This is especially important in Britain and other left-hand-drive countries. Also, bicycle and cart traffic may flow against auto traffic in some locations.

5.20 Do look out for possible assault from a bicyclist or motorbike rider. This is important if you are walking out in the open in a park or on an uncrowded sidewalk. Don't carry your packages or purse in a way that makes them easy to snatch.

5.21 Do use a taxi for going long distances to unknown parts of town. Have the hotel doorman negotiate with the taxi driver to wait for you at your destination, if it is a place or time that taxis are not easily available. Don't pay your fare until you return to the hotel. It may be useful to have a reliable tourist agent, concierge, or hotel manager—or your client/customer/host—to suggest a reliable taxi driver or service that could be available for the duration of your visit. Where there is a terrorist threat, a taxi hailed in the street or one negotiated for by a trusted intermediary, such as your host, is the most secure (see also 4.23).

5.22 To purchase a newspaper or get a shoeshine, go to a place that is off the street, where the public cannot see you pull out your wallet. Buy a paper or get a shine only from vendors inside restaurants or otherwise off the street.

5.23 If attacked, put your bag or briefcase between you and your attacker. Use your bag as a shield. If your bag is the object of the assault, let go of it, so that your attacker will not stab or hit you. Back away and call for help.

5.24 Read the local newspaper or an English-language daily. It is important that you know about local crime or political developments that might affect your security.

Special Problems for Women and Men Traveling Alone

5.25 If you are a woman without an escort, your problem may be more than just detecting the presence of someone following you in the street. The problem may be how to get rid of him (or them). If the situation seems threatening, get off the street into a store, or hail a taxi. If police or park guards are nearby, call for help, and identify those who are causing the problem.

In most countries, there are standard female replies—of varying vehemence—to insulting or suggestive male comments, proposals, or initiatives. ("No," accompanied by a cold shoulder, is pretty safe for starters.) Your customer/client/host can probably catalogue the likely comments and the appropriate response to each. The hotel receptionist may also be helpful on this issue.

5.26 The same tactics apply for a man who becomes the target of homosexual attentions. However, the areas in major cities where such attention may be expected are usually known and thus avoidable.

A Note on Hostile Surveillance

5.27 As a fearful traveler, you can become paranoid and waste a great deal of time needlessly trying to spot nonexistent surveillants. A professional surveillance team would have many members, supported by auto and communications backup, so that not even a security specialist—much less a traveler in a strange land—would be able to detect its presence. As a short-time visitor, it is most unlikely that you would attract such an investment of time by host government security forces, terrorists, or criminals. The instructions in this guide are intended only to get you to look for what is fairly obvious and apparent. A pair of pickpockets will be looking for the conspicuous tourist leaving the hotel, and they will have to get near you to do their work. If you are inconspicuous, and if you look over the crowd as you leave the hotel, chances are that the pickpockets will follow someone else. Just the same, if you have observed the features, hair, and shoes of a person loitering near the hotel, you are likely to notice this person if you see him standing beside you at a news kiosk or a museum entrance in another part of town. If you do see the same person, make sure your passport and valuables are in a safe pocket, and follow the other precautions given here. However, don't let attention to someone's shoes distract you from an uninterrupted look at the rose windows of Notre Dame de Paris, and don't let your fear of imagined surveillance prevent an additional business call (see also 5.14 and 5.54).

Dos and Don'ts for Automobile Security

5.28   Don't drive a fancy, conspicuous car or limousine, especially one that has company or "official" markings. If you rent a car, avoid American makes, and select one that is common in the street. This precaution is especially important if you are going to a remote or isolated area. Also, consider renting a car in each major city that you are visiting, so that, for example, you will not have Madrid license plates in the separatist Basque area of Spain.

5.29   Don't leave valuables, such as a purse, within sight from the street. Put your purse, camera, or tote bag on the floor, not on the dash or by the back window or on the seat beside you. Don't wear jewelry or a watch that is visible from the street.

5.30   Keep your car windows closed and your car doors locked while stopped at a stop light. This is especially important in urban areas, where you might be assaulted from the curb.

5.31   Don't stop for accidents you see on the road, especially in isolated areas; They might have been staged. The frail young lass waving for you to stop to help fix her flat tire may have friends hidden behind the car. If you must slow down at the scene of an accident, try to keep moving; if you must stop, leave yourself room to maneuver.

5.32 When you are coming to a stop, always leave at least half a car length of space between you and the car (or barrier) in front, so that you have room for an evasive maneuver. At a crowded downtown intersection, plan what direction you might go if someone on a motorbike broke a window and tried to grab your watch. Be prepared to drive on the sidewalk if necessary.

5.33 When you are stopped in traffic, always keep your car in gear, and be ready to move or take evasive action quickly.

5.34 In congested areas, drive in the left lane. It is more difficult to be pulled over from the left lane. In a terrorist attack, the car to your right would have only the rear window to shoot from. At a stop light in an urban area, it is probably best to be in the center lane of a three-lane road, so that you are protected from anyone on the curb.

5.35 Park off the street at night. It is best to park in a garage that has an attendant, where strangers won't have access to your car.

5.36 Always lock an unattended car, and hide all luggage from view or put it in the trunk. Make sure that you put your luggage in the trunk before arriving at your parking place, so that no observer will see you put it there.

5.37 Don't leave your car with an unknown attendant. This is often a difficult requirement, but the attendant should at least be part of the hotel staff or clearly an employee of the parking establishment.

5.38 When parking on the street, try to avoid a spot that is near a kiosk, wall, or shrubbery that could hide an attacker on your return. By the same token, as you approach your car parked in the street or in a parking lot, look around to see that no one is in a position to assault you. You are especially vulnerable as you stoop to put your key in the lock; you should look around carefully before you do so.

5.39   Before you get into the car, look in the back seat to be sure that no one is hidden there.

5.40   In high-risk areas, or in areas where you may have serious problems if you get into an accident, hire a driver or get a limousine service (with an inconspicuous car). Often, your customer/client/ host will offer to drive you or have someone from the firm drive you to see the sights or go to a nearby scenic village. Such an offer should be considered carefully. It may be unwise to borrow your host's car, even if it comes with a driver. Remember that if your host has been the target of surveillance, you become the target in your host's car.

   Note: A professional auto surveillance team in a large city will have many members, radio communication between cars, and, probably, zoned assignments so that detection of constantly changing autos would be difficult even for a security professional. As in the case of foot surveillance, such auto surveillance is a big investment for a government security force, terrorist group, or criminal group and is probably not warranted by your visit. If you are traveling in an area where a fast or new car might be conspicuous and you suspect that you are being followed, a standard detection technique is for you or your driver to make four right turns around the block, then four left turns. If the trail car is still with you, drive to the nearest police station or U.S. mission. Bear in mind that such a tactic will tell your trailing suspect that he has been spotted and might provoke an attack if the original intent was to harm you or the owner of your car.

Terrorism: How to Avoid Becoming a Victim

5.41   As a foreign traveler, your best defense against terrorist attention is anonymity. This defense is weakened by any publicity that may attend your visit and by the increasing number of people who know of your visit. In addition, if you are visiting with "the right people" and making contacts at "the right level," you are probably associating with the very people who are the target of terrorist attention. For this reason, for the duration of your visit, your host's or business associates' security problems and precautions become your security problems and precautions.

5.42 Unless you are visiting an overseas branch of the company you represent, you probably will not be in a position to review your associates' security plan. However, your pretravel investigation (see 1.87, 1.88, and 1.98–1.109) will have prepared you with information about the nature of the threat and about where you should (and should not) be staying in town. Additional precautions can make you an elusive and inaccessible target for terrorists. For the most part, the following precautions apply to long-term residents as well as travelers, so they also will serve to test your local host's security plans.

Dos and Don'ts for Averting a Terrorist Threat

5.43 Don't establish a pattern of activity that is observable by surveillance or easily known to the hotel staff. In going about your business, vary the times and places you have meals, business meetings, and recreational activities. Avoid a repetitive routine; change the routes you use to and from meetings, lodging, and other activities every day. Once your schedule of meetings has been set, review it to see whether there is a pattern that might be observable.

5.44 On an extended visit, avoid all pattern and routine. If you are going to be in one city for several months, and your main pattern of movement is going to be a daily trip from your hotel to a particular office, change your departure times as much as an hour either way, and change your routes so that you arrive at the hotel and office from entirely different directions at different times. If terrorists are trying to observe you, this will tend to force their attention near your office and lodging, which must be the places you are best protected. The objective is to become such a nuisance that terrorists will chose easier prey.

Note: Attempts to avoid routines and exposure have sometimes resulted in greater danger. During the spate of business executive kidnappings in Argentina in the 1970s, many foreign companies had their executives reside in Montevideo, Uruguay, a forty-five-minute flight across the Delta. A bomb placed on any Friday afternoon flight to Montevideo or any Monday morning flight to Buenos Aires would have been a sure-fire hit.

5.45   Avoid publicity, news interviews, and especially photo or TV coverage. This assures that terrorists will have less opportunity to know that you (or representatives of your company) are in town and to know what you look like. Have your talk with the dignitary being photographed at a business reception after the media have left or when they are interviewing someone else.

5.46   Avoid unneccessary public association with those who are likely and conspicuous terrorist targets. If your meeting with the U.S. consul general or the local director of Citibank lasts until late, don't accept an offer to be dropped off at your hotel on the way home. The conspicuous armored car and escort lead car full of armed bodyguards will draw attention to you as you get out at the hotel. If you feel obliged to accept such an offer, ask to be dropped off at some other point, such as a restaurant (one that you don't frequent) near the hotel.

5.47   Don't let the hotel staff or the office staff know your schedule or plans in advance. Your schedule should be information restricted to your family, to those traveling with you, and, perhaps, to your customer/client/host. Those who set up your schedule—perhaps the secretary in your client's office who is telephoning to make appointments because you don't speak the language—should be cautioned not to give out details of the rest of your schedule (such as "You can meet immediately after the 9 o'clock conference with Mr. X at the Bank of Boston").

5.48   Don't delegate authority for setting up your schedule too widely. Don't have the hotel clerk do your telephoning for you, and don't allow unknown office staff members to do it.

5.49 Where you might be a terrorist target, don't be alone in public places, even in your hotel. Go with others to the hotel restaurant, as well as to restaurants outside the hotel, and to any show or event. There is safety in numbers.

5.50 Always maintain the initiative in setting up meetings or making appointments. If you make the call and determine the time and place, this allows you to vary the pattern as you wish and prevents you from being set up for a prearranged, widely advertised meeting in exposed surroundings. If your overseas office is to set up your schedule and make appointments, make sure that some blocks of time are left open and that they consider your schedule from a security standpoint.

5.51 Maintaining the initiative is critical when there has been publicity surrounding your visit. If advance publicity is important in your business, there should be a screening procedure for unknown prospective clients, and the times and places of meetings should be your choice. If your overseas office, or that of your host, is secure, meetings should be set up there.

5.52 Build some element of security into prescheduled activities. Make sure that the prescheduled dinner party given in honor of your visit is in a secure location, not in an outdoor restaurant. If you attend a Chamber of Commerce lunch that is always held the first Tuesday of the month (and you know that the U.S. ambassador is to speak), come late and leave early. Try not to play golf with your company's chief executive on Saturday morning at his club if you know that he plays there every Saturday morning. Plan to have additional security at the overseas plant on the day you are planning to inspect it or make a widely publicized visit.

5.53 In public places, such as a restaurant, sit where you cannot be seen from outside and try to sit on the far side of a column, a wall, or structure from the entrance. Especially in well-known restaurants frequented by foreigners, sit at a table away from the entrance, so that you cannot be seen through the front window or door. You want to be out of the line of fire and protected from any bomb blast. These same precautions should be taken at hotels, at clubs, and even sitting on the deck of a yacht in the harbor. If there is a bomb blast, don't go to a window or try to inspect, since a second blast may be planned to hit those who come to look.

5.54 Be alert for any indications of surveillance, especially when you arrive and leave your office and your lodging and when you are with others who might be targets. A surveillant will have to have some excuse for staying in a public place for an extended period and waiting to spot you. Common "covers" for such unnoticed waiting include posing as lovers in a parked car, as street vendors, as telephone or utility repairmen, or just as loiterers. If there seems to be a pattern, or if you regularly see the same car or face, call the police or call a U.S. consular officer and ask how to contact the proper authorities. If you have been conscientious in observing other precautions, you will be likely to force any surveillants to find you near your lodging or near your office—that is where you must be most alert (see also 5.14 and 5.27).

5.55 If you need more guidance than is provided here, you probably need professional help. There are political risk companies that provide instruction in detecting surveillance, and there are courses in countermeasures designed for busy executives. There would seem to be a point, however, at which managers and sales executives are no longer doing their jobs effectively if they take the time to become security experts. Your insurance broker or travel agent can refer you to security firms (see also 1.125 and 1.134, especially item 12).

Host Government Problems

5.56 If your business is one that is frowned upon or considered illegal by the host government (for example, buying up foreign antiques or selling securities to nationals holding expatriated funds), it is probably not wise for you to visit that country at all—or, in any case, this is the wrong guidebook for you. However, there are situations in which you might attract official attention even when your intentions are legal and aboveboard. For example, Brazilian military authorities followed the representative of an American warplane manufacturer to see who he was contacting besides the designated Brazilian Air Force officer. In Argentina in 1975, an American executive representing a multinational (non-U.S.) oil-drilling company was tailed by authorities who wanted to know who he contacted. If, for some reason, your customer/client/host in the country is under government scrutiny, your association may direct the scrutiny to you.

There have also been other situations in which American travelers have been acted against by local authorities. For example, several American businessmen were detained by police in a massage parlor bust; American tourists were arrested at a black market exchange house; police detained an American at the scene of an auto accident when the local driver convinced the police that the American, who spoke only English, had caused the accident.

5.57 In some countries where foreign business and tourism is a major source of revenue, the embassies, hotels, and congregating points of foreign visitors are policed by plainclothes security personnel. Thus, the casual loiterers you may spot on leaving your hotel may be "white hats," not "black hats."

5.58 If you are arrested or taken into custody by police, ask to call your embassy. This is where your list of emergency numbers is important. If the circumstances are threatening and there are onlookers, throw out a business card or a handful of cards and shout for anyone in the crowd to call the U.S. Embassy to report your problem. International conventions provide for your right to call your embassy, however, so continue to request, politely, that you be allowed to do so.

5.59 Because problems with host governments are unusual situations for travelers to encounter, there is no standard list of dos and don'ts. In planning your security measures, however, you should consider circumstances that might put you at odds with the host country authorities (see also 1.124).

Anticipating Random Dangers (And What to Do)

Hotel Fire: Step-by-Step Safety Procedures

5.60   There are standard procedures for you to follow during a hotel fire (see also 4.12 and 4.13):

- Put your hotel room key where you can reach it when you get out of bed. If you smell smoke, grab the key and keep it with you.
- If you have a smoke hood, put it with your key and keep it with you (see 2.12 and 3.12).
- If you smell smoke, try to call the fire department or police for help—not a hotel security guard. If you speak the language, tell the fire department or police representative what room number you are in. If you cannot reach the fire department, call the hotel desk; remember to tell the clerk your room number.
- Feel the doorknob before opening the door. If it is hot, don't open the door—there may be fire on the other side.
- If the doorknob is not hot, open the door a crack and peek out. If it is not too smoky, go to the fire exit (to which you will have memorized the directions, number of doorways, and location of handrails). Close the door behind you.
- If there is smoke but no fire, crawl to the exit—with your eyes closed, if necessary (you will have memorized the way). Carry a wet washcloth in your pocket to cover your mouth in case the smoke becomes too thick for you to breathe.
- Don't use the elevator; it is a death trap.
- Keep your key handy in case you have to retreat to your room.
- If the doorknob is hot and you have to stay in your room, open the window if there is fresh air outside. Don't break the window, because you will want to be able to close it if there is smoke outside.
- Fill the bathtub with water and soak towels and sheets. Stuff the wet towels and sheets around the door and any other openings to the inside of the hotel. If the bathroom has a vent, turn on the fan; if it doesn't work, block it with wet towels.
- Use a wet washcloth over your face to protect yourself from inhaling smoke. Wait for help.

- If you have a smoke hood, it will enable you to tolerate smoky conditions for a limited period. You should still crawl below the smoke for visibility.

Shooting in the Street

5.61 If your estimates of the political stability of the country you're visiting were wrong and trouble starts, you may have to deal with emergency situations. The following advice from journalists describes what to do when shooting—not necessarily aimed at you—starts in the street:

- When the shooting starts, lie down flat and cover your head with your arms; don't look up until the shooting has subsided. Then get away as fast as possible.
- If you are in your hotel when shooting starts, stay away from the windows, turn out the lights, draw the curtains (to show that the window is not being used to shoot from), and put a mattress or upended bed against the window.
- If possible, get out of the danger area. If that is not possible, try to determine where the shooting is coming from (by the noise) and put yourself on the far side of a wall from the shooting. The safest place in a building under fire is in a lower story, in an interior bathroom or stairwell.

How the U.S. Embassy Can Assist You When You Need Help

What the Embassy Will Do for You

5.62 The embassy can issue you a new passport to replace one that is lost or stolen. The consul will issue a replacement passport for the standard $42 passport issuance fee. If you are destitute and cannot afford the fee, the consul may issue you a temporary passport that will be valid until you return to the United States. If you cannot adequately establish your identity and U.S. citizenship, the consular officer will cable the Department of State, at no expense to you, for instructions.

5.63 The embassy can help you find medical services, including an English-speaking doctor, in case of injury or illness. It can also inform relatives or friends about your situation and ask them for guidance or funds (see also 1.45). However, you would probably be better off seeking guidance from your customer/client/host.

5.64 The embassy can help arrange for the return to the United States of the body of a deceased traveling companion or family member.

5.65 The embassy can help destitute American travelers contact relatives, friends, bankers, or employers and can advise them on the best way to transmit emergency funds. The consul can also tell you how to inform the police about stolen funds or inform American Express about lost or stolen traveler's checks. U.S. officials will contact the Citizen's Emergency Center in Washington, D.C., where arrangements can be made for your funds to be wired to the embassy or consulate. Funds will be made available within twenty-four hours of receipt by the embassy or consulate, which *may* advance you some emergency funds until your wired funds arrive.

5.66 The embassy can provide restricted aid in a dispute that could lead to legal or police action and can provide a list of local lawyers and help you find adequate legal representation. As in the case of medical assistance, your customer/client/host may be a better source of legal references than the consul, although this will depend on the kind of legal problem you have. (New American Express and Blue Cross–Blue Shield insurance programs also provide ready legal references; see 1.50 and 1.52.)

5.67 The embassy will help locate missing Americans and will help Americans during local civil unrest or natural disaster. One of your first steps on arrival should be to register at the U.S. Embassy so that consular officers can locate you in an emergency. This is a must in a trouble spot, but it is not as necessary in an untroubled (not disaster-prone) country, especially if you have a tight schedule.

5.68 The embassy will help an American who is being detained by local authorities by visiting in detention; notifying relatives, employers, or friends; finding adequate legal representation; attempting to get relief if conditions are inhumane or unhealthy; and paying for (on a reimbursement basis) emergency medical care, food, and supplementary diet items.

What the Embassy Will Not Do for You

5.69 The following are services the embassy will *not* provide for U.S. travelers abroad:

- Give or lend money or guarantee or cash personal checks
- Provide direct legal representation or advice
- Serve as a travel agency, information bureau, or bank; search for missing luggage; settle disputes with hotels; help get work permits or jobs
- Act as couriers or interpreters
- Provide bail or get you out of jail
- Arrange for free medical or legal services

The Embassy's Role in Terrorist Hostage Situations

5.70 United States policy in regard to terrorist hostage situations, even when American diplomats are involved, is to hold the host government responsible for the peaceful resolution of incidents, to avoid direct negotiations with those holding the hostages, and to refuse to pay ransoms for the release of American citizens.

This official policy masks a wide range of activities, ranging from conversations with the host government and its security forces, to behind-the-scenes negotiations with terrorist go-betweens, to rescue operations.

5.71 If you determine that there are serious grounds to believe that terrorists are planning activities against you, you should contact the consular officer at the U.S. Embassy and ask for assistance in contacting local authorities.

Other Embassy Services of Use to Travelers

5.72 The commercial attachés at the embassy can provide a wide range of useful services to a business traveler (in addition to services provided in the United States by the Commerce Department to aid U.S. businesses doing business abroad):

- A commercial library that includes most local and U.S. trade publications
- A file of business references for Americans doing business abroad
- A correspondence file of complaints about local businesses, usually from American businesspeople who have had bad experiences

Note: If you or your company is the victim of sharp or illegal business practices, one of your recourses is to write up an account of the problem and file it with the commercial attaché. The commercial attaché will not pass on mere hearsay about local businesses, but can provide accounts of business transactions and allow others to draw their own conclusions.

If you establish a working relationship with the commercial attaché's staff, they may give you some hints in private conversation, regarding which local businesses should be dealt with carefully, what the local payoff practice might be, and where bottlenecks can be expected in the flow of trade.

This office can also be a good source of references to contacts in local financial institutions, other Americans doing business in related lines, and government ministries that could be helpful in conducting your line of business.

5.73 The economic affairs officer of the embassy, who often represents the U.S. Department of the Treasury as well as the Department of State, is often well informed about the general economic situation of the country and can be a good source of background information and, perhaps, references to banks and financial institutions and to finance, economic planning, and central bank officials in the government.

5.74 Depending on the nature of your business, the agricultural attaché and/or the U.S. AID Mission representative may also be of assistance to a business traveler.

5.75 The embassy will provide notary services to Americans abroad.

Assessing the Embassy Role When You Need Help

5.76 In asking for help at a U.S. Embassy, you should remember that foreign service officers—especially senior ones—are paid and promoted for establishing and maintaining good relations with host governments. To the extent that your situation may upset relations between the embassy and the host government or local authorities, you represent a "problem" to the embassy. Unless you are a prominent American, an embassy officer will have little interest in bailing you out if all his negotiating "chips" with the host government must be spent on your behalf.

    Note: U.S. consuls—as opposed to U.S. foreign service officers acting as consular officers or embassy duty officers—are in their own professional promotion "cone" within the State Department and are evaluated and promoted, in part, on their ability to serve Americans in distress. Although you should expect a professional job from the embassy, do not expect resourcefulness or fervor.

5.77 A communication from your office in the United States or from your family at home to your representatives in Congress can do much to heighten the embassy's attention to your plight. However, don't use political pressure unless you really need it; it may not go down well with the embassy officer who may be the key to your salvation. It is also a good idea to tell your representatives in Congress about the effective work of an embassy officer; there may come a time when the lion will need Androcles' help again.

Everyday Problems You May Encounter

Cultural Differences

5.78   If you have ever lived overseas, you have discovered that the pace, values, expectations, and terms of reference are different in each country and different from those in the United States. Deadlines and promptness may be considered relative terms, and an efficient phone system or a reliable electricity supply may not be a high priority. The process of negotiation may involve many face-to-face encounters to establish a basis of confidence before the real business at hand can be mentioned or discussed. You may even find that American business "virtues" are held in disdain and that forthright presentations are regarded as bold effrontery. You should also observe and copy local behavior regarding how close you should stand to a person in conversation and whether it is acceptable to touch someone, even in a gesture of friendship.

5.79   In Latin countries, where the legacy of Roman law places the burden of proof on the citizen/applicant, the importance of documentation and the intrusive role of the bureaucracy is a source of irritation and frustration to most Americans. In such countries, you must have a birth certificate (notarized, translated, and certified by a consulate) to show that you are who you say you are for purposes other than a short visit (even though you have a passport), a marriage certificate (notarized, translated, and certified by a consulate) to show that you are married or that you are the parent of a legitimate child, and a power of attorney (same authorization requirements) from the other parent to travel as a single (especially female) parent of a minor child—or divorce papers or a death certificate (same authorization requirements) for a minor child's father. For each new application—to rent an apartment, to enroll children in school—all the same documents must be supplied anew. As one Argentine lawyer commented: "You are always having to prove that you are not an elephant, and there is always one last document missing."

5.80 Even for a seasoned traveler, these cultural differences may become exasperating. They require understanding and adaptability. For example, you may have to spend a great deal of time waiting for a dial tone—and then get the wrong number. It is important to remember that your foreign business counterpart, if he is at all perceptive, may use your impatience or frustration to his advantage by going slowly when you are up against departure deadlines. It is thus essential that you maintain a sense of humor and a flexible attitude while holding to your own professional standards. The best course is for you to research the foreign culture and business mores before you meet them head on.

5.81 The following publications deal with problems of intercultural business negotiations:

1. *International Negotiation: A Cross-Cultural Perspective,* by Glen Fisher (1980), available from Intercultural Press, Inc., 70 W. Hubbard Street, Chicago, IL 60610. This excellent, brief primer on the subject gives specific examples of differences in negotiating in Japan, Mexico, and France.
2. *Going International: How to Make Friends and Deal Effectively in the Global Marketplace,* by Lennie Copland and Lewis Griggs (1983), available from Random House, Inc., 201 E. 50th Street, New York, NY 10022, for about $20. This comprehensive book—organized by topic, such as "sales" or "negotiation"—contains much useful information for American companies doing business abroad. However, it does not give detailed foreign examples to demonstrate each topic and thus is often too general.
3. *Do's and Taboos Around the World: A Guide to International Behavior,* compiled by Roger E. Axtell for the Parker Pen Company (1985), available by writing the Parker Pen Company, P.O. Box 1616, Janesville, WI 53547, for about $8. This book is packed with useful worldwide cross-cultural dos and don'ts. The table of contents could be improved for fast reference. High points are the international gesture dictionary and a country-by-country guide to protocol, greetings, and dress.

Accidents, Mishaps, and Delays

5.82 The crises most likely to afflict international travelers have little to do with assaults or terrorist bombs. The most likely problems are mundane. Examples drawn from the experience of one traveler include:

- A twelve-hour delay for jet engine repair in a remote town, with no other flights to anywhere
- Checked baggage lost by the airline for two weeks
- A broken fan belt on a rented limousine on a little-traveled road late at night
- Cleaning fluid used on a business suit by the hotel giving a fellow traveler a painful rash on his legs
- Wife hospitalized when a collapsible chair at a country club collapsed with her in it
- A fellow business traveler being severely sunburned and requiring treatment in a clinic for several days
- A fellow business traveler nearly drowning in the undertow at a crowded beach
- A rural town hotel that wouldn't accept any form of payment except cash—and funds could be wired only on a weekday

Mishaps invariably happen on Sunday afternoons or evenings. The only preparation for such mishaps is psychological. Have a good book handy for inevitable waiting in lobbies, airports, and on mountain passes.

6
Heading for Home: A Checklist to Ensure a Safe Trip

The Final Days of Your Trip

Reconfirming Your Reservation

6.1 Within seventy-two hours of departure (or in some cases within twenty-four hours) go to the airline office and reconfirm your flight—or have the concierge do it. It is better to do this in person, not by phone, so that you will have the confirmation on your ticket, not just on the airline computer. If you reconfirm by phone—or someone does it for you—note the time it was done and the agent's name. In some cases, failure to reconfirm within twenty-four hours will result in your being bumped and having to pay an additional fare. This should be checked carefully by your agent beforehand (see also 4.6).

6.2 If you need to reschedule your flight at the last minute and the local airline office is not open, you may wish to call your travel agent in the United States for a flight that is likely to be crowded (see also 1.86). You might also try to call the airline office in some other city, where the office may be open (see also 1.86).

Getting Ready to Go

6.3 You have done all the things on your list, sent your telexes, written up all your meetings, seen and photographed all the sights, eaten at all the recommended restaurants, bought presents for every member of your family, sent postcards to friends and office staff, and said your good-byes. All that remains is to pay your hotel bill, take a cab to the airport, and board the plane for home. In your relaxed mood, you should not forget the precautions regarding exposure in public places and the potential terrorist threat at the airport or on board the plane. Both TWA Flight 847 from Athens in 1985 and Pan Am Flight 73 from Karachi in 1986 were ultimately U.S.-bound flights.

Checking Out and Paying Your Hotel Bill

Allow Lead Time

6.4   Tell the hotel desk of your departure beforehand, and pay for the last meal separately, so that the final, complete bill can be prepared in advance. When you go to pay your bill, leave plenty of lead time to find a taxi and get to the airport. When you are in a long line at the cashier's window, there is invariably someone ahead of you with a problematical bill.

Review Your Hotel Bill

6.5   Be sure to review your hotel bill carefully, not only to see that the charges are proper but also to ensure that the categories of expense suit your accounting needs. Hotel bills in Paris, for example, may list all beverages, including orange juice or bottled water, as "bar" bills. If your company does not reimburse you for drinks, you may want this difference noted on your bill.

Pros and Cons of Using Cash or Credit Cards

6.6   Ask beforehand what the exchange rate will be for the hotel bill. It may be to your advantage to pay in U.S. dollars (or with a U.S.-dollar credit card) or to exchange dollars elsewhere (at a better rate) and pay in local currency.

Since credit card billings may not be processed for a week or more, and credit card services use the exchange rate on the day they process the bill in the United States—not the rate on the day you pay the bill—if the dollar is falling in value relative to local currency, you should exchange currency at the higher present value and pay in local currency.

If the dollar is increasing in value relative to local currency, it is better to use your U.S.-dollar credit card, because the exchange rate will be more favorable when the bill is processed in the United States than on the day you pay the bill. Bear in mind, however, that American Express and some other credit card companies charge a 1 percent fee on all foreign exchange transactions. Credit card companies use various methods to calculate the rate of exchange, but the rate used is always the one in effect when they process your bill—long after the day you signed your credit card receipt.

6.7 Save a dated newspaper clipping of the official dollar exchange rate on the days you had major transactions with your U.S.-dollar credit card—especially in a fluctuating exchange market. (This is more convenient than looking for back editions of the *Wall Street Journal.*) From time to time, American Express and other credit card companies use exchange rates on their bills that are totally out of line—and never in your favor. When you get your credit card bill, run through your records to see that the foreign exchange rate used makes some sense—allowing for a week's fluctuation. Major errors can usually be adjusted in a phone conversation with the credit card company billing office.

Packing

6.8 Review 2.30–2.37 regarding what to carry on your person or have readily accessible in your hand luggage. You should have the following close at hand:

- Enough foreign currency to pay the airport taxi and any local embarkation tax at the airport (usually also payable in dollars)
- Any exit document you were given on entry to be returned as you leave
- Your sales receipts for items to be declared to U.S. Customs (also, in France, such receipts show the sales tax, which may be

reimbursed to you by French authorities on presentation of the receipts)
- Your doctor's certificate for any unusual drugs, to be shown to U.S. Customs

6.9   Review your luggage, briefcase, daily records, and address book as if you will have to explain their contents to terrorists during a hijacking (see also 2.12 and 2.13).

Preparing for the Trip to the Airport

6.10   Call the airport to find out whether your flight will leave on time or whether it will be delayed.

6.11   By the time of your departure, you should have worked out procedures for getting a "safe" taxi (see 4.23 and 4.24). Follow those procedures, or call a limousine to take you to the airport.

Curbside to Boarding

Protection from Crowds and Confusion

6.12   As you get out of your taxi and pay the fare, there are likely to be crowds and confusion. You will be putting your wallet or money carrier back into your pocket in full view of people in the crowd. Make sure that all your valuables are in safe, buttoned pockets or in a zippered pocket of your hand luggage (see also 4.1).

Get Off the Airport Main Concourse

6.13   After presenting your ticket and checking your luggage (see 3.1–3.7), get off the main concourse and into an enclosed area. If you are a member of one of the airline traveler's clubs, go to the club facility, or go through customs and get into a protected area. This will protect you from pickpockets and from any terrorist assaults or bombs on the concourse, where access is often unrestricted. If you go shopping or to a restaurant at the airport, try to stay away from the main concourse.

Safety on the Flight Home

Review sections: 3.8, The Safest Seats During Crashes, Fires, and Terrorist Incidents; 3.9, Terrorist Hijackers' Initial Focus on the Cockpit; 3.11, Emergency Crash Landing and Evacuation Procedures; 3.19, What to Do During a Terrorist Hijacking.

6.14 The experiences of TWA Flight 837 from Athens and Pan Am Flight 73 from Karachi seem to indicate that travelers should try not to sit in the very front of the airplane and should try to delay identifying themselves as American citizens as long as possible. Put your U.S. passport in your hand luggage, so that if you are told to leave your seat by a terrorist, you will not have your passport with you—and you will have a valid reason not to have it with you when it is requested (see also 3.8–3.20).

7
Arrival in the United States

U.S. Customs

7.1 Customs regulations are detailed in the U.S. Customs Service publication *Know Before You Go,* available free on written request to the U.S. Customs Service, P.O. Box 7118, Washington, DC 20044, and at any U.S. Passport Agency Office. Only a select outline is included here.

7.2 For convenience, consider mailing items purchased abroad to your home in the United States. Gifts valued under $50 may be mailed to the United States; they should be clearly marked "unsolicited gift—value less than $50." You may receive one such package per day without paying duty. Dutiable items may also be sent by mail; duty will be collected by the mail carrier at your door. Such customs regulations are described in *International Mail Imports,* available from the U.S. Customs Service, P.O. Box 7118, Washington, DC 20044, and also by calling your nearest U.S. Customs Office. The security of foreign mail service from pilferage where you are visiting *may* be an issue to consider.

Unaccompanied-baggage departments of major airlines can also handle the mailing of such items. This alternative is often time-consuming, however. Packages must be boxed according to local requirements, or documents must be filed with an unaccompanied-baggage forwarder to show, for example, that your rug is not part of the national heritage. Also, you will have to go to an airport or Customs warehouse in the United States to pick up the items after you return.

A Quick Guide to U.S. Customs Regulations

7.3   There is a $400 exemption from duty for anyone who has not used the exemptions within thirty days and has been out of the country for at least forty-eight hours (otherwise, the exemption is only $25). The next $1,000 of items is dutiable at a flat 10 percent rate (so that the total duty on the first $1,400 of items will be $100). The $400 exemption may include 100 cigars and 100 cigarettes and one liter of alcoholic beverages (not for minors). The excess value on hard liquor will be taxed at 10 percent—less for wine or softer liquors.

Restrictions

7.4   *Know Before You Go* (see 7.1) details restrictions on the following items:

- Agricultural items
- More than $10,000 in U.S. or foreign currency, traveler's checks, securities, or negotiable instruments
- Art treasures or artifacts (especially pre-Columbian articles)
- Drugs containing narcotics (have your doctor's certificate or prescription ready)
- Wildlife and fish
- Other specialized items, as listed in *Know Before You Go* (see 7.1) and other customs publications. For details, call the U.S. Customs Service, in the U.S. Government listings in your local metropolitan telephone book.

Prohibitions

7.5   The following items are prohibited:

- Illegal drugs, narcotics, toxic substances, liquor-filled candy, absinthe
- Agricultural products that might injure U.S. crops
- Endangered species and their by-products (for example, a tortoiseshell comb)

- Obscene publications
- Other specialized items (see customs publications)

Declarations

7.6 Your objective is to get through customs expeditiously—possibly without opening a suitcase. The best way to do that is to fill out your declarations form completely and honestly and to have all the declared items in one suitcase—with receipts at the ready. In general, U.S. duty rates are so reasonable and the consequences of misrepresentation are so dire that it is not worth the risk to try to hide anything on your customs declaration form. In most cases, customs agents are reasonable about innocent oversights in filling out your form—unless there is an apparent pattern of deception. Bear in mind that customs agents have probably seen every trick under the sun.

It is wise not to go through customs decked out like a Christmas tree, laden with gold watches, cameras, and liquor just purchased at the duty-free shop. Nor should you flaunt valuables that you took with you in the first place—especially expensive photo equipment. (You may have to prove that you had them with you when you went abroad.) Declare such items, but put them in a suitcase.

Financial documents that might appear to have a value greater than $10,000 should not appear on top of the pile as you open your briefcase. Again, declare according to the requirements, but don't invite questions unneccesarily.

Preregister items on Customs Form 4457—Certificate of Registration for Personal Effects Taken Abroad—which must be presented with the items and a completed form for certification by U.S. Customs prior to departure. If you are carrying much camera equipment of *foreign origin* with you on your trip, preregistration with Customs may prevent delays and a search for historic purchase receipts later.

Home Again: A Final Checklist

7.7 Remember to mark your calendar in the United States so that you take your malaria pills for six weeks after your return.

7.8   Remember to check the foreign exchange transactions on your credit card bill to see that you are not being unfairly overcharged. If you have good records and a strong case, a phone call to the credit card billing office will usually result in an adjustment.

7.9   A comprehensive outline of the tax code provisions that cover foreign business travel is provided in the appendix to the *1987 Guide to Personal and Business Travel,* published by the National Institute of Business Management and available from Research Institute of America, Inc., Department 204110, Mount Kisco, NY 10549, (914)241-7500, for $5.50 (including postage) per copy. An update incorporating the latest tax code provisions is expected.

Index

About the Author

P eter Savage is the director of an international trading company that has exported American equipment and conducted market surveys in Europe and Latin America. He was based in Argentina in the 1970s when mounting political unrest and terrorism resulted in a military coup, ushering in the government counterterrorism known as "the dirty war." Previously, he was posted with his family in Brazil by the U.S. Foreign Service at a time of increasing terrorist activity, including the kidnapping of the United States ambassador and assassination of a United States military attache. Mr. Savage graduated from Harvard College and the University of Pennsylvania Law School and received a Fulbright Scholarship to Brazil.

Metric Equivalents

Quick Guide to Metric Equivalents

1 meter   = 3.28 feet
1 kilometer = .62 mile
1 kilogram = 2.2 pounds

Celsius temperature $\times$ 1.8 + 32 = Fahrenheit temperature

Linear Measure

1 centimeter = 0.3937 inch
1 inch   = 2.54 centimeters

1 meter   = 39.37 inches = 1.0936 yards
1 yard   = 0.9144 meter

1 meter   = 3.2808 feet
1 foot   = 0.3048 meter
1 mile   = 1609 meters
1 kilometer = 0.62137 mile
1 mile   = 1.6093 kilometers

Square Measure

1 square meter   = 10.7636 square feet
1 square foot   = 0.0929 square meter

1 square meter   = 1.196 square yards
1 square yard   = 0.8361 square meter

1,000 square meters = 11,960 square yards = 1 hectare
1 hectare   = 2.47 acres
1 acre   = 0.4047 hectare

Temperature Line

C	F
100	212
90	194
80	176
70	150
60	140
50	122
40	104
37	98
30	86
20	68
10	50
5	41
0	32
−10	14
−20	−4
−30	−22
−40	−40